Flamethrowers

Guardians of the game

Volume 2
Polar Bear Lacrosse

Based on the comic "Flame Boy" written by Brody Childs

D0448252

J. Alan Childs

Savage, Minnesota USA

ISBN-13: 978-1535544726
ISBN-10: 1535544724

Acknowledgements

I would like to thank those who helped inspire me to write and encouraged the concepts in this story.

To my family and friends who have shared this adventure with me, thank you.

A special thanks for my long-suffering editor, Cindy Wilson. Her endless work on teaching me the art of writing seems to have no bounds.

Flamethrowers

Guardians of the game

Volume 2

Polar Bear Lacrosse

For my grandchildren

Contents

1

Polar Bears

Tyson was excited for his first hunting trip. His brother, Osseo, had hunted with his dad for several years, but now Tyson was old enough. His dad always said, *you need to be double digits to hunt.* And last week Tyson had finally turned 10 years old.

It was fall and the traditional time to hunt caribou and gather enough meat for the long winter ahead. Tyson wanted to learn everything from his father about how to hunt their food.

Tyson grew up in the small town of Winston, located in the arctic, along the shores of Hudson Bay. Tyson's family has lived there for as long as they could remember. Many generations had watched the polar bears migrate from land to winter ice to hunt and eat.

Tyson's father Blade was a big man, strong and rugged, with dark skin and long black hair. Osseo, Tyson's 14-year-old brother, was starting to look like their dad, growing taller and his black hair becoming longer.

"Tyson, you ready?" called out his dad. "We have a long day ahead of us; make sure you have everything packed."

"Just getting all my stuff in my bag," answered Tyson. "Do I get to shoot today?"

"Not today. We talked about this. You're going along to watch and learn," said his father.

Yuraa, Tyson's mom, was packing the last items for the trip. Yuraa was a small but stout woman who grew up in the arctic like her husband. She also had long black hair and strong hands developed from tanning hides, making clothing for her family, and living in this rugged land.

Osseo loaded the final items onto his snowmobile. He had been on these trips before and knew how to keep warm and safe. It was early October and snowstorms could hit anytime, plunging the temperatures well below zero.

But for now, the weather was good: above zero and clear skies. A good day to hunt a herd.

"Tyson! Hurry up. We need to leave," said his father.

Tyson grabbed his pack and handed it to his dad to pack onto the snowmobile, then hopped on behind his dad. It was a long trek and Tyson would not be riding on his own snowmobile today.

Yuraa stood by as she watched her husband and boys leave on their expedition.

There was fresh snow on the ground, but not so much that the snowmobiles would have to work hard. The arctic tundra is flat. No trees, no mountains, no cover.

Blade liked to run the snowmobiles fast on the open tundra, and Tyson enjoyed the thrill of a fast ride. He moved the snowmobile from side to side to make Tyson hold tight. Blade was proud of his sons and he was going to teach them the ways that his family had taught him.

They rode for about an hour and came to a hill where they could see down into a shallow valley. Osseo stopped and signaled to his dad to stop as well. Below was a herd of caribou.

"Look Dad," said Osseo. "They are still here."

Osseo and his father had been there a couple of days before, scouting the herd.

Looking around, Blade saw that they were mostly alone. Mostly, because up to their left were three polar bears hanging out. The bears seemed to be snacking on some brush sticking out of the snow. They only rely on plants when they are desperately hungry.

The boys knew this was the dangerous time of the year for polar bear attacks. Polar bears, unlike their cousins to the south, were pure meat eaters, unless they ran out of food. Polar bears primarily eat seals, but other sources like walrus can serve as a meal too.

Polar bears do not hibernate in the winter. Nope, winter is when they can eat and get fat, feasting on seals through the Hudson Bay ice.

Tyson remembered last winter when his dad took him out on Hudson Bay to watch a polar bear hunt and eat a seal. Tyson saw how strong the polar bear was, smashing the ice with his paws to create a hole to hunt from. Then the bear just sat there, waiting for a seal to rise to the surface to breathe.

Tyson watched as the polar bear reached in with both paws to grab a young seal and pull it up onto the ice. On ice the bear has the advantage and can kill and eat the seal. Ice is an ally of the bear, because the seal cannot move fast on the ice.

Tyson watched the bear bite the seal, but turned away as the blood flowed from the squealing animal.

His dad then grabbed Tyson and urged, "No. You must watch this. The bear is a powerful and skilled warrior. We learn by watching, and learn respect for what they can do."

Tyson watched the mighty bear as he slowly ate the seal. The ice became blood red and so did the bear as he feasted.

"You see the size of the seal," said Blade. "He is no bigger than you. And when he gets hungry in the fall, you're gonna look like a nice seal meal. So you don't go near the bears in the fall."

Tyson's mind raced as he continued to watch the bear eating the seal and realized that his dad was right. That seal was the same size as him.

Osseo called out to his dad, "Should we move on and get away from the bears?"

"No," answered his father. "This is a good spot. They seem content."

Blade then turned to Tyson and started to explain how they picked which caribou to shoot. Why they were up on a hill looking down at the herd. Tyson listened as his dad taught him how to not scare the herd, find the right animal they needed to feed themselves this winter, and how to feel the wind and understand how it could help or hurt their chances.

Osseo was listening too. He had heard it before, but he liked listening to his dad tell the stories about how he learned to hunt and why the Creator gave us the animals to survive.

"Osseo," called out his dad. "Have you picked one for us? Can you see the one?"

Osseo was a little surprised his dad asked him for advice. Dad always picked the animal to shoot.

"Yes," said Osseo. "I see a young one, not too big yet. He is on the left side."

Osseo had learned from his dad to hunt the young teenagers in the herd. The antlers would not be too big, but this was not a trophy. This was food for his family for the harsh winter months.

"Okay son, it's your shot," said Blade.

Osseo took the binoculars from his eyes and

looked at his dad. Was he really giving him the chance to shoot his first caribou?

"It's your time," said his father. "Your turn to provide for the family. Show your brother what you have learned."

Osseo looked at Tyson, who stared back with excitement and pride in his older brother.

Blade and Tyson looked through binoculars as Osseo aimed towards the herd. Blade was reminding Osseo where to aim, and how to breathe, when he heard pounding on the ground. He thought the herd was moving. "They're moving. Take your shot."

But Blade was wrong. It wasn't the caribou herd that was moving. It was one of the polar bears running right at them.

Blade grabbed Tyson and pulled him up and behind him, putting himself between his son and the bear. Tyson struggled to get his feet under him because his dad had pulled him up so quickly. Tyson's feet slipped and he started to slide away from his father.

Blade jumped up and flung himself down the icy slope towards Tyson. His instinct was to not leave Tyson alone. Tyson was frantically grabbing at the snow to slow himself down. But his gloves and snow suit were slippery and it was tough to stop. Tyson reached, grabbed, clawed - trying everything to stop himself.

Finally Tyson was able to dig in his boot and stop himself. His father reached him quickly and grabbed Tyson's arm, lifting him up.

Suddenly Blade realized he had left Osseo on the ridge alone. Osseo had stayed down as the polar bear passed over him towards Tyson. But now he was alone and the bear turned his attention to Osseo. Osseo was scared; he knew he had to react. Instead, he froze. His father yelled to him, "Shoot him! Shoot him!"

Blade knew that Osseo had his gun ready to shoot the caribou. But his son was not moving or firing his weapon. Blade knelt down and shot quickly, hitting the bear in shoulder. The shot only seemed to annoy the bear. Blade began to run up the hill, trying to distract the bear. Loudly yelling and waving his arms, he reached the ridge and the bear started to retreat.

As the bear wandered away, Blade knelt down to see how his son was doing. He was clearly shaken, not reacting to his touch.

Then Blade heard the scream, "Help, Dad!"

Blade turned. The bear had started wandering

towards Tyson. "What should I do?" yelled Tyson.

Blade raised his gun to shoot again, but if he missed the shot, he might hit his son. He couldn't risk it. He started down the hill again, telling Osseo, "I'll be right back. I have to help your brother." Osseo did not respond.

Blade ran towards the bear again. Tyson was moving down the hill, trying to keep from falling. Blade now had a shot and he took it. The bullet hit the bear in the same spot on the shoulder, but this time the bear roared in pain.

Blade made more noise, trying to scare off the animal. The bear retreated down the hill towards the caribou herd, which was now thundering away from them.

Tyson ran to his dad and hugged him. This was more excitement than Tyson had expected. He looked up at his dad and asked, "How's Osseo?"

There was a scream. This time it was Osseo. The two other polar bears had heard the sounds and were now running at Osseo. Osseo was running, too, but in the opposite direction. He disappeared over the ridge, towards the snowmobiles.

"NO!" yelled Blade. He grabbed Tyson and started running back up the hill. He knew Osseo could not outrun them. With Osseo and the polar bears out of sight, he could not use his gun to help his son.

Osseo kept running towards the snowmobiles. He was not sure if he would make it, but he thought he had to try.

Osseo started screaming. There were no words, just yelling as he fell down. Blade and Tyson reached the top of the ridge. Tyson looked to see both bears on his brother. Tyson dropped to his knees seeing blood, just like that day on the ice with the seal.

Blade ran towards the bears shooting wildly, hitting them. But it was too late.

2

Departure

Yuraa heard the sound of a snowmobile approaching. She looked out but saw only one snowmobile, and in the sled she saw Osseo, not a caribou.

Yuraa ran outside, looking at Osseo's body, covered in blood, and his clothes ripped to shreds.

Yuraa turned to look at her husband. "What did you do?" she cried out.

Blade was slow to respond. His heart was heavy with the loss of his oldest son.

Yuraa did not wait long for an answer. She broke down and began hitting her husband with her flailing arms, weeping, and crying.

Tyson stayed on the snowmobile, scared and alone. His brother was dead. His older brother, who had watched over him and had taught him so much, was gone.

Eventually Tyson moved off the snowmobile, and his mom realized he was there, alive. She ran to him. "Are you okay? Tyson are you hurt?"

Tyson was feeling responsible; he started to think it was his fault for falling down the hill, making his dad leave Osseo.

"It's my fault mom," said Tyson. "I fell down the hill and…" Tyson's voice failed him.

Hearing his son say this broke Blade's heart. "Tyson, how can you believe that? It was not your fault! We should not have been hunting there. We saw the bears and we should have moved like Osseo said."

Yuraa was furious at hearing her husband's confession. "You saw bears?" she began, "And you stayed to hunt anyways? You killed our son?"

Blade hung his head. He knew. It was on him. He did not defend himself against her attacks. She was right. He too blamed himself. The loss of his oldest son was his fault.

At the funeral, Tyson and his mom listened to stories from Osseo's friends. Blade did not attend. He could not bring himself to face his son in death.

As Tyson returned home from the funeral he found his dad packing. "Where are you going?" asked Tyson.

"I need to leave for a little while," said his father.

"I know Osseo is dead, but I'm your son too," bellowed Tyson. "I need you."

Blade did not hear his son's pleas for him to stay.

Blade looked at his wife. She did not look like she could forgive him. He walked past her and started to say something, but nothing came out. He could feel her anger and emptiness. She said nothing in return as he left.

Tyson followed his dad to the snowmobile. Tyson yelled and called for his dad not to leave. But Blade started the snowmobile.

Blade took off, leaving his son behind. Tyson chased him down the road. He ran, and ran, and ran, until he could no longer feel his legs. He collapsed, and watched his dad disappear out of sight.

It had been two years since his dad left and Tyson was now twelve. It had not been easy on Tyson with his brother and father gone.

Growing up in a town on the edge of Hudson Bay, Tyson was used to seeing polar bears. But now it was just a reminder, every day, of the attack that killed his brother and had driven away his father.

Although polar bears rarely attack people, Tyson had learned that they can and sometimes do. This knowledge had, over the last two years, turned to fear. Tyson was terrified of them and angry about what they had done to his family.

At school the bullies teased Tyson about his fear of the bears. They knew it was his weakness, and like all bullies do, they preyed upon those fears. Last year they trapped him outside the school near the dumpsters, where two polar bears were looking for food. Tyson screamed for help as the bears paid him no attention, eating the trash. But the laughter from inside the school was humiliating. The whole school saw his fear.

Recent summers had grown longer. The polar bears were growing more dangerous, because the ice was too thin to hunt on. The bears stayed in town and roamed around looking for scraps of food. Something someone might have left out. Something they could eat. A polar bear relies on its fat to survive the cold winters. A skinny polar bear does not last long on the ice.

But this danger never slowed the kids from teasing Tyson and making him more and more afraid. His dad taught him to ice fish, hunt seal, and even hunt whale by watching the polar bears. But it was now this same animal that haunted him.

Tyson had grown used to being alone and took to going for long walks or for rides on his snowmobile. He lived with his fear, and kept a good distance from the polar bears. What he liked was visiting the places his dad had taken him to. He would often visit the ridge where his brother had died.

One fall afternoon after a fresh snowfall, he took off on the snowmobile towards the ridge. He sat there for hours watching the herd of caribou below.

He remembered how excited he had been to be with his dad and his brother on the hunt. As darkness neared he knew he should start heading

15

home. But the silence and stillness and sunset colors on the snow were so peaceful that he wanted to stay, just a little longer.

It was dusk and the sun was dropping quickly below the horizon, making it harder to see. A quick flip of a switch and the headlights came on.

Just as the lights brightened the path, he realized that he was not alone. There was a large polar bear wandering the path along the trail.

Tyson felt the fear rise within him. His heart pounded, and he felt hot all of a sudden, then cold and sweaty. He could hear his pulse, and felt himself start to shake. His mouth felt dry. Then just as suddenly, he began to feel anger. He tightened his jaw and narrowed his eyes, glaring at the bear.

He could hear the voices of the kids from school calling him names, mocking him, and laughing at him.

Rage was building inside him. He remembered that his dad had told him he had to face his fears. But his dad had left. He hadn't face his own fear. Tyson was tired. So tired of being afraid. The anger. The rage. Finally it had reached a place where it boiled over and he had to do something.

Tyson started his snowmobile, slowly approached

the bear, then turned away. He taunted the bear by going at him and turning away, quickly enough to not get hurt.

But this was not taking the anger away. In fact he was getting frustrated. He had to do more.

He started talking to himself. *You took my brother. You took my dad.*

Tyson started to circle the polar bear. He continued to taunt the animal, getting closer and closer.

Tyson drove up the big hill. He sat there. He felt something burning inside him. He wanted to hurt the polar bear. *You hurt me, now it's my turn to hurt you.*

Tyson took off his helmet. He wanted the bear to see him. To know who he is. Then Tyson drove his snowmobile down the hill, straight at the polar bear. Faster and faster the snowmobile went, gaining speed. Tyson screamed to the bear, "You are not going to scare me anymore!"

The bear growled loudly at Tyson as it maneuvered itself out of the way of the snowmobile.

Tyson had missed.

As Tyson turned around, his speed was so fast that the snowmobile flipped and Tyson flew into the snow.

The polar bear was now upset.

Tyson saw that his snowmobile skis were broken, and he was forced to abandon the machine. But his feeling of rage had not changed to fear. Instead, he stood to face the bear.

"Okay, here it comes!" screamed Tyson.

3

Park

The park in Brenton was beautiful this time of year. The leaves in late September made the park alive with color, while the grass still had a wonderful green look. White Crane had just arrived at the park to meet Kenny, Casey and others playing lacrosse.

White Crane showed the kids his special lacrosse

stick that featured a shiny white pearl color with special feathers.

He then asked Kenny to join him on an adventure.

"Wait. What do you mean we need to go?" asked Kenny.

"The polar bear stick has been found. They are going to need our help," said White Crane.

"Who are *they*?" asked Casey.

"I'm not sure actually," answered White Crane. "We'll meet them when we get there."

"Wait. Where is *there*?" again asked Casey.

"Casey, I had forgotten how inquisitive you are," said White Crane. "We are going to a town called Winston, near Hudson Bay."

"Dude, that's in Canada!" said Fred.

"Yes it is Fred," said White Crane. "We need to leave right away. Kenny, you need to go home and pack."

"Mr. Crane, with all due respect, we can't just leave town," said Kenny. "Our parents aren't just going to let us go driving up to Canada. Alone."

"Sure they will Kenny, they let me go to hockey tournaments up there all the time," said Fred.

"We won't be driving," said White Crane. "The

only way to get to this town is train or plane. There are no roads where we are going."

"No roads?" Casey was startled. "Exactly where is this place that we're going to?"

"Wait. Who said *we,* Casey?" asked Kenny.

"What does *that* mean?" answered Casey.

"Everybody just calm down and let me explain a few things," said White Crane.

"Winston is a small town on the edge of the Hudson Bay. It's where a large number of polar bears live, and hunt on the bay in the winter. The town there is home to a small village where they live among the polar bears. The village is above the tree line on the frozen tundra of the arctic. There are no trees, no mountains, and not much for food either."

"Now Kenny, I need you to help me with whoever has found this powerful stick. The person who has it will have the strength of the polar bear. Your friends are welcome to come but the travel will be difficult."

Kenny and Casey looked at each other and realized this was not a decision they could make on their own. Their parents were going to have a say in this, whether they liked it or not.

"We will need to talk with our parents before we

can agree," said Casey. "Kenny, we better start at your house first. My mom will be a lot more agreeable if your parents say yes first."

Casey looked at Kenny, who was clearly not on board with this himself. "What it is?" asked Casey.

"Do you think we can really go with him?" asked Kenny. "I mean, that's a long way from home."

"White Crane needs our help. He's asking for our help," said Casey.

Kenny looked at White Crane, who was busy talking with others about Hudson Bay.

"Okay," said Kenny, trying to convince himself that everything was going to be okay. "We can do this."

Kenny and Casey hopped into the limousine with White Crane.

As they rode in the limo, Kenny looked down at the stick in his hand; the owl stick, the stick that had changed his life and the community. Kenny thought to himself, *Do I really need to do this? Is someone really in trouble? How far will this go?*

Kenny looked up from his stick; he was feeling bad about what he had said to Casey. Looking at her he said, "I'm sorry about saying you shouldn't go with us. I want you to go."

"It's okay," said Casey. "I'm not sure we can go anyways. Do you really think your parents will let you leave town?"

"Maybe they'll make my older brothers go," thought Kenny.

White Crane, who was looking up into the sky through the sunroof, turned to Kenny. "Enough of this *maybe* talk. We are going. This is not a choice you have. You are a Flamethrower. You have a responsibility. There is no maybe. We will convince them together."

They pulled up in front of Kenny's home in the long white limousine. Kenny's brother Tommy came out to see what was going on and why a limo was in front of his house.

Ryan was back at the University of Minnesota attending college. Tommy, still in high school, was excited to see the limo. When Tommy saw Kenny get out of the limo, his face dropped.

Tommy had assumed it was one of his friends coming by for some special event. "So Kenny, what is this? Forget your way home?" taunted Tommy.

But when Casey and White Crane also got out, Tommy knew something was up. Kenny looked concerned and worried about something. "Mom,

Kenny's home," called Tommy.

Kenny's mom walked out of the house to see Kenny and Casey near the limo. "Well, don't you two know how to make an entrance," teased his mom.

"Hi Mrs. C.," said Casey.

White Crane started walking towards the house. Kenny's mom recognized him, but had not seen him for a few months. "Haven't seen you around for a while Mr. Crane."

"It is my loss," said White Crane as he moved towards her, reaching out his hand. "Beautiful day isn't it?"

"Come in and tell us why you are here," said Kenny's mom. She glanced at Kenny to get a read of his face. *What's going on? Why is White Crane visiting our home?* She had not seen him since the hospital when her husband was injured.

Kenny was not looking up, and clearly she knew he was not comfortable with whatever was going to happen next.

The kids sat down close to White Crane. Kenny asked his mom, "Where's dad?"

"He's in town running some errands," she answered. She knew he was stalling, but wanted to get the conversation started.

"So, Mr. Crane, what brings you to our home?" she asked.

Kenny started with a brave voice to show this was his idea. "You remember what happened in the spring and the stick I found?"

"Of course," she answered quickly.

"Well, there are more sticks and people need our help," said Kenny.

"I see," she said. "And what does 'need our help' mean'?"

"Well." Kenny paused. "Well…you see…" his voice started to trail off.

Casey jumped in, "Other sticks are being found. And since we know what to do they need us to help them."

"How can you help them?" asked Kenny's mom, as she could tell where this was going.

Casey answered, "We can show them how the sticks work, how to find the evil stick, and White Crane can protect us." Casey was the nervous one now.

White Crane could see Kenny's mom was going to need some convincing. He could tell she did not understand what the kids meant to say.

"Mrs. Conley, when we talked a few months back I told you the story of the Flamethrowers. How they came to be and how Kenny had come across one of the hidden lacrosse sticks. I know it's hard for many to believe these stories, but you saw first-hand how much damage these sticks can do."

"I'm not really sure what I saw," replied Mrs. Conley. "I only know that my husband was hurt and Kenny was running around town causing damage. And Briggs hurt a lot of people.

"Then you showed up, and tried to tell us it was all part of a big plan of some kind," she continued. "I am not sure I want Kenny to be a part of any more stories."

White Crane leaned forward. "Kenny has become a part of something bigger than himself. He has an obligation to fulfill his duties as a Flamethrower."

"Duties!" Mrs. Conley echoed. "Kenny has no duties outside of this family."

Suddenly the front door opened and Kenny's dad, Cody, walked in. White Crane stood up and Kenny and Casey jumped up too.

"Hi Dad," said Kenny sheepishly.

"Wow this is quite a sight, White Crane in our living room, and a limousine in our driveway," said

Cody. "What are you three conspiring to do?"

White Crane reached to shake Cody's hand and said, "Good to see you again, sir. We have an adventure to take and I need your son to go with me."

"Adventure you say," said Cody. "And where would this adventure be to?"

"Winston, near Hudson Bay," answered White Crane.

"Canada?" exclaimed Kenny's mom. "You didn't say anything about leaving the country."

"We haven't had the chance Mom," said Kenny. "We need to help someone. This is important."

"Hold on, hold on," said Cody. "Somebody get me up to speed on what's going on here."

Kenny and Casey looked at each other. This was not going well. They looked to White Crane, who knew he had to take the lead.

"The story I told you about the Flamethrowers is true. Other Flamethrower sticks are being recovered from their rest. The sticks are powerful and the people who find them may not know the stories and what to do with them. They will need our help to guide them."

"A stick has been found in Winston. This is a very

powerful stick and very dangerous to anyone who has possession of it. Given our experience with the sticks we have been asked to come and help the people in this town."

"Do you know these people?" asked Cody. "Do they really need your help?"

"Yes, I know them and I have visited them before," answered White Crane. "They will provide a place to stay and feed us. You will have no worries about their safety, I will watch over them."

"Them? Who else is going?" asked Kenny's mom.

"Casey is going with us," answered Kenny.

Cody looked back at White Crane. "What can Kenny really do to help you? I mean, he is so young and not experienced in much outside of our hometown here."

"He is stronger than you think, sir," said White Crane. "Besides, I am not that young anymore and I need the help. I promise I will return him as soon as I can."

Kenny's mom was pacing now. She said, "Kenny can't go. It's fall and school is starting soon."

Casey jumped into the conversation. "School doesn't start for another two weeks. Remember it's late this year because of the fire."

There had been a wildfire in the area in August and several building had fire damage. The school district decided to delay the start of school until mid-October.

Cody looked at his wife, who was staring down White Crane. Cody touched her arm to get her attention. "This could be good for Kenny. If they are still on break and he has a place to stay…"

She cut him off. "It's winter already up there. You know how cold it might get. Besides, how will you get there?" she asked, turning back to the group.

"We have a ride to Winnipeg, then we will catch the train to Winston," said White Crane. "I have the tickets here." He reached into his pocket and held them out.

Kenny and Casey looked at each other, thinking the same thing. *We have tickets?*

"Maybe Ryan or Tommy should go along to help out?" asked Kenny's mom.

Tommy came in from the other room, saying, "I am not going on some babysitting trip with these two. They've cause enough problems for me."

White Crane chimed in, "I appreciate the thought, but the more people we have, the more difficult it will be to manage. Casey and Kenny can handle what

29

needs to be done."

"You promise to bring them back alive, and in one piece, right?" asked Kenny's mom.

"You have my word," said White Crane. "Kenny has much to look forward to."

"Casey, does your mom know you want to go?" asked Cody.

"No," said Casey, looking at the floor.

"Well, I guess I can call her," said Mrs. Conley.

"Does that mean I can go?" asked Kenny.

"Now listen," said Cody. "Mr. Crane is in charge of you two. You are to listen and follow his instructions at all times. No challenging his authority. DO NOT LEAVE HIS SIGHT."

Casey started towards the stairs, saying "I'm gonna help Kenny pack, then we can go to my house."

White Crane nodded.

As Kenny and Casey went upstairs, Cody turned back to White Crane. "Exactly what do you get out of this? This adventure. I don't really believe this story you're telling us. But I know what I saw last spring, too. I can't deny Kenny has some weird connection with that lacrosse stick."

White Crane looked at Cody with a steady stare.

"I believe the stories of my ancestors. I cannot explain in modern terms how this all works. But there is a change coming to our world. We are going to be a part of this change."

White Crane turned and walked outside.

Flamethrowers II

Train

Kenny and White Crane were sitting in the limousine outside of Casey's house. They both knew it would be easier on Casey if they didn't go in. Holding the owl stick in his hands, Kenny was looking at the detail of the bone and the carvings.

Kenny asked White Crane, "Who made these sticks? I mean how did they make these sticks? This must have taken a long time."

White Crane did not respond. He was again

looking up through the sunroof into the sky, watching a hawk above.

Casey ran out of the house yelling back at her mom, "See you soon, love you."

Kenny looked out at Casey's mom. It was normal for Casey to spend a lot of time with his family, but that was for hockey, or recently lacrosse. Now she was going without the rest of the Conley family. That was not normal, and Kenny saw that worry in Casey's mom's face.

Casey brought her bags to the back of the limousine and handed them to Little Joe. She asked, "You going with us to Winston?" Casey remembered the first time they had met Little Joe, in front of the Red Hawk casino while trying to find White Crane. He was a huge man with massive hands, but was a kind and gentle giant.

"No," answered Little Joe. "I am dropping you off at the train station in Winnipeg. I have family near there, and will wait for your return."

"I'm ready," said Casey as she got in the back with Kenny and White Crane. "My mom's a little freaked out, but your family did a good job of convincing her it was okay."

"She doesn't look too convinced," said Kenny.

"Okay, convinced is maybe too strong of a word, but I'm going," said Casey. She was clearly excited to be heading out on an adventure of her own.

Little Joe hopped in up front and the limousine ride to Winnipeg began.

The city of Benton is located on the Iron Range, which is the northeast section of Minnesota. The trip was about 5 hours to Winnipeg, passing by several towns they had played hockey in: Warroad, Baudette, Roseau, and others.

As they reached the border there was a little distraction with the border patrol. Kenny and Casey had their passports, a requirement for most Minnesota families who crossed the border for fishing trips, or hockey tournaments. It was more that they were not traveling with their families. A couple of phone calls were made, and soon enough they were in Winnipeg.

Little Joe got out of the limousine as they arrived at the train station. Casey, Kenny, and White Crane hopped out and stretched after the trip.

"Good luck," said Little Joe as he handed White Crane the luggage tickets. "Let me know when you arrive back and I will return you home quickly."

"Thank you," said White Crane.

The train was boarding and Kenny and Casey hopped on to find a good spot.

The three sat together and settled in for a long trip. "How much farther is it?" asked Kenny.

"It's another 800 miles north," said Casey. "I checked and it takes almost two days on this train."

"What? Two days?" complained Kenny. "I know we keep asking, but exactly where are we going?"

White Crane began to describe the area. "We are going to one of the first settlements on Hudson Bay. This area is known for its relationship with the animals there. People followed the example of the polar bear, learning to fish and hunt on the bay. The winters are long and hard, while the summers are short and beautiful."

"You mentioned there are no trees," said Kenny.

Casey answered, "Yes, we are going above the tree line. It's an area that doesn't get enough sun, or warmth to support trees. It's an open area where there is nothing to stop the wind or cold. It can be brutal for people to live in."

"So why do people live there?" asked Kenny.

Casey looked at White Crane as if to say *your turn.* "There is a connection there with the animals and the sea that is very different. We all live in areas we have grown used to over the generations. People live together for many reasons. Seeing the mighty polar bear walk around your village I'm sure is very special to them.

"Polar bears are very different from the bears we have in Minnesota. Most bears are omnivores, meaning they eat plants and some animals. But they are typically lazy, so they eat whatever is easiest, like plants, berries, and roots. When fish are easy to catch they will eat them. Then they will hibernate in the winter.

"The polar bear is the opposite of those bears. There is not much vegetation to eat. So they are mainly meat eaters. They especially like seals. But they will eat what they find too. Like a whale carcass, walrus, or other large animal.

"Polar bears have a very keen sense of smell. They can smell an animal from miles away. They can swim for miles at a time between ice sheets. And they are most active in winter. Unlike the black or grizzly bear they do not hibernate. The winter is when the ice forms on the bay and makes the best time to eat, and save up body fat for the short mild summers when they cannot hunt as easily."

"So why do you call them dangerous?" asked

Casey.

"They are powerful creatures, sometimes standing over 10 feet tall and weighing over one thousand pounds."

"Wow!" said Kenny. "But they don't attack people, right?"

"It is true that polar bears don't like humans and stay away. But the world is changing. The summers are getting longer, and the ice takes longer to form. The bears get hungry waiting for the ice to be ready for hunting. The bears eat the human garbage first, but guess what you look like to a polar bear? A nice plump young seal. A hungry polar bear can be very dangerous, and you need to respect them. Stay away from them."

"Do you think we will see any on this trip?" asked Kenny.

White Crane answered, "This is the fall and they are waiting for the Hudson Bay to freeze up. They will be making the trek to the shoreline near the village, waiting for the ice."

"So you're saying this is the most dangerous time to be around polar bears," said Casey. "The time when they're hungry and in the village."

"Yes, that is what I am saying," answered White

Crane.

"I think you left that part out when you were talking to my mom," said Kenny.

"We will be fine Kenny," said White Crane. "We have friends who will be helping us. They will show us what to do."

"Oh yeah, you mentioned them before," said Casey. "Who are they?"

White Crane had talked enough. He answered, "We all could use some rest. We will need our strength when we arrive."

Kenny and Casey sat back in their chairs and drifted off as the scenery went by out the windows. Kenny noticed lots of trees, a river, and some light falling snow. Not so different from Minnesota, yet.

Casey woke up as the train made noise as it entered a bend in the track. She sat up to see a large moose in a field paying them no attention. She sat staring at the moose as Kenny started to wake up.

"Where's White Crane?" Kenny asked.

"Not sure, I just woke up," answered Casey.

"How do you think we are going to find this polar bear stick?" asked Kenny.

"I'm sure White Crane has a plan," answered

Casey. "I have no idea where we'd start."

"Maybe the friends will already have it when we arrive," hoped Kenny. "He seemed to avoid your question when you asked him about who's going be there to meet us."

"Yeah it's strange he didn't want to talk about it," said Casey.

"I wonder why we he brought us," said Casey. "If he has friends up here why would he need us to come along? There's something he's not telling us."

"Yeah like it's polar bear starving season," responded Kenny. "Mom wouldn't have given any okay knowing that."

White Crane returned, bringing snacks.

"Hungry?" asked White Crane. "It's moose jerky."

"Yeah...I just saw a moose. No thanks," said Casey.

Kenny took one. He wanted to ask White Crane about his friends again, but tried a different approach.

"What are some of the stories of lacrosse in this village?" asked Kenny. "They must have some experience since they have the stick."

White Crane looked at Kenny with a thoughtful face. But he answered, "There are many stories of lacrosse being played by all people on Turtle Island. In this area, once a player moves on to the next world it is said they can be seen at night still playing in the sky."

Kenny and Casey looked at each other in confusion. Kenny asked, "You mean after they die?"

"Yes, the players can be seen at certain times of the year, as the days grow shorter. They appear as green, blue, yellow, and other colors playing lacrosse in the sky to entertain the Creator. It's a privilege to play lacrosse up here."

"You mean the Northern Lights?" asked Casey.

"Yes, of course," said White Crane. "That's what you call them. We call them our ancestors who still play the game."

"Will we see them while we're here?" asked Kenny.

"Not sure if we will Kenny. It's a bit early in the season to see them."

"We see them in Minnesota too," said Casey. "But I never heard them referred to as lacrosse players before."

Kenny grew impatient and jumped in to interrupt them. "Who are we meeting in Winston to help us?"

Casey paused, as she wanted to know the answer

too. They both stared at White Crane, awaiting his answer. He stood up to leave when Casey reached up and added, "Please."

White Crane grinned and said, "You are persistent, I'll give you two that. We are meeting the elder of the nation there. His name is Journey, and I met him many decades ago. His people are struggling with many changes in the world, like the polar bear. They have new struggles and their way of life is considered old and outdated to many."

"Does he know who has the stick?" asked Casey.

"I don't know," answered White Crane. "I haven't talked to him yet. We left on rough terms last time I was here."

"Wait, hold on," said Kenny. "He doesn't know we're coming? I thought you said he would help us?"

"He will help us," said White Crane. "And he knows we're coming. It just hasn't come from me that we are on the way."

Kenny and Casey were more confused than when they started asking questions.

5

A Stranger

A stranger stopped as he heard a faint sound in the distance. He paused to listen carefully. He heard a snowmobile crash and a polar bear howl. The stranger started his snowmobile and went towards the sounds.

Tyson, seeing his snowmobile was broken, turned to see a very angry polar bear. But Tyson was upset too. This creature was responsible for breaking up his family. For killing his brother. Now he had put himself in this situation to deal with his hatred, his fear.

Tyson walked slowly towards the polar bear, yelling.

"You killed my brother!"

"You took my father!"

"I hate you!"

Tyson's anger was starting to blind him. Blind him to the fact that this bear was many times his size and only wanted to be left alone. But Tyson didn't want the bear to run away. He wanted to hurt this animal for all the things some other bear had done to his family.

"I hate you!"

"You ruined my life!"

"I am going to kill you!"

Tyson began running at the bear; running and screaming towards the very thing that had killed his brother. Tyson had no weapon, no tools, and no rational reason to be doing this.

Tyson felt the cold in the air. It was cold like the day his father had taken him hunting, the day that had changed his life. What had he done wrong? His brother and dad had hunted before without any issues. But this time he was with them. It must have been him that had caused the bears to attack.

Closer and closer he came. His only weapon was the sound of his voice yelling at the bear.

As he drew close, the polar bear stood up on his hind legs to show how big he was, to scare and intimidate Tyson. But Tyson was not scared away. He did not care that he was in danger. He just wanted revenge.

The polar bear was not sure what Tyson wanted. The bear was not used to smaller creatures attacking it.

Then a new sound caught the bear's attention. It was an engine, a loud engine. Tyson turned and a snowmobile pulled up between him and the polar bear.

Who is this? thought Tyson in frustration. *What is going on?*

"Hop on kid," said the stranger. "I'll get you out of here."

Tyson shook his head and said, "NO!"

Tyson turned to run away from the snowmobile but in the chaos he had lost track of where the bear was. He ran away from the snowmobile but right into the bear's path. The bear had decided he'd had enough and was charging at Tyson.

Tyson tried to turn around but it was too late. He was too close to get away from the bear.

WHAM!

Tyson's arm seared with pain. The polar bear's claw had slashed right through his jacket, sending blood spewing into the air.

Tyson got up and started to run away from the polar bear. But the bear was fast and quickly gained on Tyson. The stranger, seeing the two running, started towards them again.

The polar bear rose up and jumped on top of Tyson who was now kicking and screaming to get the bear off. Tyson could feel the weight of the bear, its anger at him. He fought back and started yelling again at the bear. But Tyson's hits and yells could not stop the bear. The bear pulled its arm back to take another massive blow against Tyson.

The stranger saw the bear on top of Tyson and drove his snowmobile directly at them. A small ridge allowed the stranger to get his snowmobile off the ground and into the air.

Just as the polar bear was moving his claw towards Tyson's head, the snowmobile hit the bear, knocking him off. The polar bear was sent flying back and away from Tyson.

Tyson struggled to roll over, but he was exhausted. He looked up, trying to see where the polar bear was and if he was going to attack again.

The polar bear got up. He was hurt. He stared at the stranger and Tyson, not moving. The bear was tired and decided to move on and leave Tyson and the stranger alone.

The stranger grabbed Tyson and tied a wrap around Tyson's arm to stop the bleeding. He loaded Tyson onto his snowmobile sled and headed into town.

The stranger pulled up in front of Tyson's home and his mom came running out. She could see Tyson was not conscience, and was bleeding from his arm. The stranger picked up the boy and walked him inside the house.

Once inside, he set Tyson down on the table and started to take Tyson's jacket off. The stranger kept his hood up and went straight to work on getting the wound to stop bleeding.

Tyson's mom asked, "What happened?"

The stranger was more occupied with Tyson than her questions. But he finally answered, "Bear," and that was all he said.

"How…where…why did he…" she trailed off. Her instincts were kicking in now. Tyson had a large gash at the top of his arm. She immediately went to work, getting her sewing kit out.

She started to sew him up while the stranger made his way out the door. He said nothing else and she was too busy sewing Tyson's skin back together to notice or care where he went.

6

Diamonds

Tyson had grown older now. It had been four years since his run-in with the polar bear. He was sixteen now, and like his father, grown tall and strong. His left arm showed the six inch rough scar where his mom had sewn him back together. He had grown his black hair long to show his strength.

Tyson wore his father's bandana. It wasn't much to look at, yet Tyson felt a strong connection with it. Tyson had outgrown most of his anger, and replaced it with a passion to become like his father.

Tyson also kept his old habits. He took long trips on his snowmobile to visit places where he had spent time with his dad.

"Mom," yelled out Tyson. "I'm heading out for the day, be back tonight."

"Tyson," she answered. "We need to get more wood chopped this weekend. Winter's coming and we need to get firewood ready."

"I know mom," said Tyson. "I got it. It'll get done. Don't worry."

With that, Tyson headed out the door to his snowmobile. He had packed a lunch and planned to be out most of the day.

Tyson rode out to the west, traveling along a road he had been down many times before. It was a cold October day with a few inches of snow on the ground. You could feel winter coming. No ice on the bay yet, so plenty of polar bears to watch out for. With a few more days at these temperatures the ice would be ready for the polar bears to hunt. Then the town would be empty of bears until the spring thaw.

Tyson continued on his way, watching the horizon getting light from the sunrise behind him. It was 10am and the sun was just coming up.

He reached the top of a ridge and his destination

was right below him. From above it looked like a spiral ring starting out wide and winding in a slowly narrowing circle, round and down, and round and down, and round and down. It was a diamond mine, built decades ago when Canadian diamonds were all the rage.

Tyson's dad used to bring him here when the mine was working and people filled the area. Tyson and his dad would sit on this ridge and watch the big machines drive up and down the mine, using the large circular road.

Tyson would come here with his brother and dad to unwind during the summer months. Tyson remembered it as a time when he and his dad spent time together.

Tyson liked to watch the great big trucks moving mounds of dirt, and hear the explosions as new holes were opened in the ground.

Tyson listened to the silence and stared off to the distance as the day drifted along for him. But the silence gave way to a voice, a very faint voice, far away.

Where is it coming from? he thought. He looked around, but the voice was so distant it was difficult to find. He kept looking around the ridge but realized it was coming from inside the mine. Way down below he saw a small image. A person was running around, and yelling.

Tyson walked closer to see what the person was yelling at. As he looked closer he could not see anyone else. Why was this person running around yelling?

Tyson began thinking the person may just be crazy, alone, and going nuts. *Better stay away* was his first instinct.

Tyson started walking back to his snowmobile. He was better off to move on. Then Tyson heard another sound. The sound was snowmobiles, and they were headed his way. Tyson looked around and could see them in the far distance.

In all his visits here alone, he'd never seen anyone else. The mine had been deserted for years now.

Tyson's instincts were to not trust anyone, so he hopped onto his snowmobile. Which way should he go? Away from the mine? He would surely be seen. Or go into the mine and hide to see who was coming? Wait...the crazy person is down below. Tyson thought for a moment. He decided it was better to hide than to be seen, so he started slowly down the ramp into the mine.

Tyson was careful not to make too much noise or move too much snow. He quickly found a cave off the path and drove his snowmobile inside to hide.

Flamethrowers II

7

Bag of Rocks

Kenny and Casey stared out the window of the train. *How much longer could it possibly be?* they thought. They watched as trees slowly disappeared. The moose, bear, and other animals became less frequent. They passed large lakes, while roads were long since gone.

The snow-covered tundra was all they could see now. Just as the train began to slow again, a large polar bear could be seen in the distance.

"Look!" said Casey. "A polar bear walking alone."

Kenny saw it. It was huge and covered with a beautiful coat of white fur.

"We must be getting close to the bay," said White Crane. "The bears look ready to hunt and eat."

Off in the distance Casey could now see some lights. She said, "That must be it. Winston."

White Crane nodded.

"Finally we're here," groaned Kenny.

As the train stopped, they stretched, left the train, and felt the cold, brisk Canadian air hit their lungs. As they found their bags they saw a large white sack with the image of a crane. They knew it must be White Crane's, but they didn't remember seeing it when they had boarded. It was bigger than Kenny, and when they tried to move it, they knew what was in it. Rocks.

Kenny had brought a few in his bag too, but nothing like this. Kenny and Casey both tried to pick it up. They could lift it but they were not going to be able to carry it.

Kenny and Casey grabbed their stuff and looked to find White Crane. They did not see him at first, but as they turned the corner they saw several people gathered around him.

"Must be the welcoming committee," said Kenny.

"Yeah, I guess," said Casey, who was distracted while trying to judge the people talking to White Crane.

The small crowd looked over at Kenny and Casey as White Crane pointed towards them. Casey was feeling uneasy about the way they looked at them, so she motioned for Kenny to stop. White Crane's voice was not loud enough to hear, but he continued to talk with these strangers.

They eventually came over to where Kenny and Casey stood.

"Kenny and Casey," said White Crane. "This is Journey, an elder here in Winston."

"Nice to meet you," Kenny and Casey echoed.

"Welcome," said Journey. "This is my son Koti and my daughter Lonni."

"Come with us, we will get you something to eat and discuss your great adventure here," said Journey.

"We found a large white bag that must be yours," said Casey, looking at White Crane.

"Oh yes," said White Crane. "Koti, can you help us with our bags?"

The group gathered the bags and loaded them into a truck. *It's cold here!* thought Kenny. *Wow, really cold.*

They pulled up in front of an old house, with small windows and surrounded by fences that were built to help block the wind.

The group made their way inside and sat down to what smelled liked wonderful soup. White Crane again introduced Kenny and Casey to a kind group of people. *The house is small. Probably to make it easier to keep warm* thought Casey.

Fireplaces were located on both ends of the room. People sat on make-shift furniture, and furs were used as blankets to keep warm. Although this house was very different from what Kenny and Casey were used to, it was a warm and comfortable place to be.

As the group sat down to dinner, Journey started the conversation. "How were your travels to our village?"

"It was very long," said Kenny.

The group around the table laughed, nodding in agreement.

"What do you think of our town here?" asked Koti. "Much different from Minnesota?"

Casey answered, "It's very different. We have a lot of trees, rivers, and some hills. It's so flat here. Like the tundra goes on forever."

Koti smiled. "Yes our land is very flat and the wind blows snow from one side of Canada to the other."

"So," Casey interrupted, wanting to get right to it. "Who found the Polar Bear stick?"

White Crane looked with disapproval at Casey. Journey too was not happy about the question. Koti had a look of interest, but waited for someone else to talk first.

"We do not share White Crane's passion or interest for the sticks. It is an old story. Some say too old. An ancient legend," said Journey.

White Crane clearly did not want to talk about this right now at dinner. He calmed the group by simply changing the conversation. "How is the ice on the bay? Can the bears hunt soon?"

Koti answered, "It is hard to tell these days. Snow has come, but the water is still warm. The ice seems to come later and later every year. The polar bears get very hungry and mean."

"We have fewer bears each year," answered Journey. "It does not look well for our village to survive if the polar bear cannot."

There was an uncomfortable quiet as everyone pondered the dilemma.

White Crane then came back to their mission. "Do you know of an abandoned mine near here? It is where we need to travel tomorrow."

Koti and Journey exchanged glances. They hesitated to answer. White Crane could tell they did not want to discuss more in front of Kenny and Casey.

The group finished their soup and White Crane and Journey walked outside to talk.

Kenny and Casey watched as they talked. Casey asked, "Why do you think they need to talk alone? I mean, what are they hiding?"

Kenny was curious too. "Do you think they already have the stick and won't tell us?"

As Kenny and Casey were watching out the window, Koti approached them. He asked, "Do you believe the stories?"

Kenny and Casey glanced at each other. "I have the owl stick," answered Kenny.

"Can I see it?" asked Koti.

"Sure," said Kenny. "Let me get it."

Kenny went to his bag to get the stick. Casey looked at Koti and asked him the same question. "Do you believe the stories?"

Koti looked down and said, "My dad told me they

were not true. Just stories, a fools quest. A trickster story."

Kenny came back with the owl stick, which was glowing in his hands. He offered the stick to Koti.

"Wow," said Koti as he reached for the stick. He studied the detail like Kenny did when he first found it. The owl bone shaft, the emblems, the head made of feathers and beaks. But as Koti grabbed the stick, the glow stopped. He watched the change with disappointment.

"Why did it stop glowing?" asked Koti.

"It's bound to the person who found it. When you touch the stick the first time it burns you, binds to you," said Kenny. "Well, at least that's what Casey told me. Actually, I don't remember much after touching the stick."

"So it's joined just to you, right?" asked Koti.

"Yep, that seems to be how it works," answered Kenny.

"Well at least until you die. Then it can be bound to someone else, right?" speculated Koti.

A chill went down Kenny's back. He glanced at Casey, who just smiled.

"What about the rocks?" asked Koti. "Are they real too?"

"Yes," said Casey. "They catch fire and explode."

Kenny was nervous about showing the rocks and the fireballs, but White Crane was still talking to Journey. So he thought, *why not?*

"Let's go outside and I'll show you the fireballs," said Kenny, feeling slightly mischievous.

Kenny grabbed a rock from the bag and led the group outside. White Crane saw Kenny coming out with his stick. The group followed and White Crane gave a nervous glance. Kenny thought if Journey didn't believe stories, maybe he could convince him with a demonstration.

"Wait, Kenny," said White Crane.

But Kenny kept walking through the cold. He stopped and placed a rock in the stick pocket. The rock started to glow. White Crane started to walk towards Kenny but Casey stepped in his way. White Crane and Journey were hiding something. Casey though that this demonstration would give them more credibility, and they could be included in more conversations.

The rock continued to get brighter and brighter until it caught fire. Seeing the fire, Kenny shot the rock high into the air and everyone watched as it fell to the ground and exploded in the distance.

When Kenny turned around, he noticed that nearly everyone in the house had come out. White Crane and Journey were clearly upset. Koti had just seen proof that the stories were true and was excited to share wit his dad.

Koti turned to Journey, "You see? The stories are true."

White Crane and Journey did not want a confrontation now, not in front of everyone. So they turned away from the group and walked inside.

Koti asked to see the stick again. Kenny handed it to him while Casey watched White Crane and Journey arguing inside.

Journey was not happy about something. White Crane continued to talk, trying to convince Journey. Casey tried to listen but the excitement from the group outside was too loud.

Koti asked Kenny for a rock so he could try. But Kenny explained that the stick would not work for others. Just like how the stick had not glowed for him.

As the evening grew late, the stories continued about Flamethrowers and possible sticks out there. Finally White Crane suggested they all get their rest for the trip tomorrow.

Kenny and Casey were getting packed up the next morning when White Crane entered the room.

"We will be going alone on our travels today," said White Crane. "Journey and the others will not be joining us."

Casey asked, "Why? I thought they would help us."

"It is not my decision," said White Crane coldly. "They have another path to follow."

Koti entered the room and said, "The snowmobiles are fueled and ready for you."

Kenny asked him, "Don't you want to go with us?"

Koti looked at White Crane as if he should answer the question. When White Crane only stared back, Koti turned to Kenny and said, "It's not my duty to go with you today."

Casey and Kenny walked outside in confusion and were soon joined by the others. White Crane was talking to Journey, who appeared to be giving him directions.

Koti approached Kenny and Casey. "The ice is very thin for the polar bears. They cannot hunt yet. Be very careful and stay away from them. This is the time they can attack, when they are hungry. Steer away from any you see."

"Okay," answered Casey. "Anything else we should know?"

Koti held out his hand to Casey. It held a white object in it. It was a large tooth. Koti said, "Polar bears do not eat their own. Our tradition is to carry part of a polar bear with us to keep safe. Here is the tooth of a large bear that died here last year. Take it, be safe."

Casey took the tooth from his hand. It was strung on a leather strap, making a necklace. She put it around her neck. "Thanks," she blushed.

As Casey turned to show Kenny the tooth, she noticed Kenny watching White Crane. White Crane had reached into the large white sack of rocks, removing a small black bag. White Crane emptied the small black bag into his hand and showed the contents to Journey. After a quick exchange and some nodding, White Crane placed the items back into the bag and handed it to Journey.

"What do you think those are?" asked Kenny.

"No idea. And since when does White Crane have something black on him?" asked Casey suspiciously.

Kenny, Casey, and White Crane finished loading

the snowmobiles and started them up. Kenny and Casey had been on snowmobiles before, but White Crane looked a bit nervous.

Despite being inexperienced on a snowmobile, White Crane led the way and Kenny and Casey followed him out of the village. The village was small, and in just a few minutes they were on the snow-covered tundra, driving west away from the rising sun.

The tundra was flat and wide open. Today it was covered with a clear blue sky, and the view seemed to go on forever. They rode for miles and still Kenny and Casey could not see any place that might be a destination. Just endless flat land, covered by snow.

As they rounded a small hill, Kenny saw an open area below. A caribou herd was huddled below, trying to eat the few remaining bushes that stuck out of the snow.

Off to the other side, Casey spotted polar bears. Three of them. One looked very skinny. She thought the skinny one was probably the scariest one because he looked the hungriest.

They kept riding, and the horizon only seemed to get farther away. As they started over the next small hill, White Crane came to a stop, followed by the others.

White Crane turned to Kenny and Casey. "We are here."

Flamethrowers II

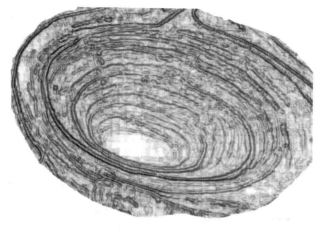

Crazy Man

Tyson watched as three snowmobiles arrived at the top of the ridge. He did not recognize the riders as being from his village. And they didn't look like people from the mining company either.

He wondered why they were here. Why come out here? He had been to the mine many times in the past couple years and had not seen anyone. Why now?

They took off their helmets and Tyson could see an old man with a long white ponytail. Next was a small blonde girl, and a blonde boy. Not exactly a scary-looking group. Still, Tyson decided it was better to stay hidden and wait to see what they were going to do.

Back on top of the ridge, White Crane set down his helmet and proclaimed, "The sticks are here."

Casey and Kenny exchanged a look that said, *how does he know that?*

Casey looked down into the mine and saw a man at the bottom of the large pit, far away. She could not make out any details, but he seemed to be moving and excitedly talking to himself, waving his arms around.

Kenny and White Crane also watched as the man ran from one side of the pit to the other.

White Crane turned to Casey and Kenny. "Let's go down, slowly. Carefully."

Kenny and Casey both nodded and hopped back onto their snowmobiles. They began to slowly move down the wide ramp. It had been created to get the oversized dump trucks in and out of the mine, so it was not a steep road.

Meanwhile, Tyson continued to watch as the three descended down the ramp. He moved deeper into the cave to stay out of sight. Tyson stood still as the snowmobiles slowly passed by. White Crane glanced into the cave, and Tyson could feel the man looking at him. He comforted himself by thinking, *it's too dark in here. He can't see me.*

Kenny and Casey looked into the cave, but did not see what White Crane saw. White Crane stopped, then walked to the entrance of the cave. Kenny and Casey both stopped, and watched as White Crane peered into the darkness.

"Did he find the stick?" Casey whispered to Kenny.

Tyson stared back at White Crane, believing he couldn't be seen. Tyson covered his mouth with his hands, trying to silence his nervous breathing.

"What is it?" asked Casey. "Did you find something?"

"Do you see something?" echoed Kenny.

White Crane lifted his hand to stop the questions. He called out into the darkness, "Why don't you come out here and join us?"

Kenny and Casey looked again into the darkness,

71

but could see nothing inside.

Tyson's heart was now pounding. He couldn't hear much else now. *What is going on? Can he really see me?*

White Crane extended his hand into the cave, saying, "We mean you no harm. Come. Join us."

Kenny and Casey continued to watch as a figure moved towards them from the darkness.

"Who are you?" asked Tyson as he cautiously emerged.

"My name is White Crane. This is Casey and Kenny."

Kenny and Casey lifted their right hands, making a small gesture of a wave.

"Who are you, young man?" asked White Crane.

Tyson looked around, not sure yet what to make of the visitors. But he answered, "I am Tyson. Why are you here?"

Kenny pointed back at his snowmobile, where a lacrosse stick was poking out of a storage pouch.

"What's that?" asked Tyson.

"A lacrosse stick, an ancient lacrosse stick," replied Kenny. "We're here to find another one. Maybe you've seen it?"

"What's lacrosse? And why are you really here?"

asks Tyson, who was feeling more suspicious.

The sound of a man yelling grabbed everyone's attention. They moved out to the road to see if the man had moved any closer. After a moment, they concluded that he was just being louder, but was still at the bottom of the mine. He hadn't yet noticed them.

Casey asked, "Do you know who that is down there?"

"No," said Tyson. "He was here when I got here."

White Crane was ready to continue the trip and changed the subject. "Tyson, why don't you join us? We're going down to investigate."

"Why should I join you?" replied Tyson defiantly. "I don't know you. Or trust you."

Kenny felt a connection to Tyson. There was something about him. He sensed that Tyson needed to join the group.

Kenny started telling the story of how he found the owl stick, the stone coffin, the red rocks, and the evil stick.

Kenny described going into the cave where the owl stick was found. About the burning of his hand as he grabbed the stick. About finding White Crane, who told them the story of the Flamethrowers. White Crane listened as Kenny told his version of the story. White Crane did not interrupt, and allowed Kenny to carry on with what he thought it all meant.

Kenny described failing in his quest to find the evil version of the owl stick, then having to face Briggs, the person who had found it. He told about his father getting injured during the battle, and how Kenny himself had to fight Briggs. In order to get the evil owl stick safely into White Crane's possession, Kenny had to seriously injure Briggs.

Kenny told Tyson how they found out about the existence of the polar bear stick, and that they were here to find it.

Tyson listened, but this all seemed way too crazy to him.

"Really?" says Tyson, somewhat incredulously. "You want me to believe this wild story about Flamethrowers, rocks, and good and evil sticks?"

Casey saw that this was going to be a challenge. She walked over and removed the owl stick from Kenny's snowmobile. She walked to Tyson and handed him the lacrosse stick, pointing to the detailed markings and asked him if he had ever seen such a stick.

Tyson looked up at White Crane. "Where are you from?"

White Crane answered, "We are from Minnesota, a long, long trip, and we're here to help."

"Help?" cried Tyson. "Who says I need help?"

Kenny and Casey looked at White Crane, hoping he would explain. But he remained silent.

Tyson looked down at the lacrosse stick in his hands. He thought to himself, *this is a really cool stick. If there is another one maybe I can get it?*

Tyson looked up and said, "Sure, I'll go with you to find this other stick."

Kenny walked over and took back his stick. Tyson noticed that as Kenny took the stick, it glowed.

Kenny asked again, "You really don't know who's down there?"

"Not a clue," said Tyson. "Like I said, he was there when I got here."

Casey went over to the edge of the spiral road to look down below. White Crane had stopped to get Tyson to join them. Did he know something she didn't? Does he know who is down there? Her mind was restless. What was next? Her mind kept racing about Journey and the secret talks, the small bag of rocks, and why they hadn't come along.

Casey walked over to Kenny as he was putting the stick back on his snowmobile, "How come nobody seems to know about this stick? I mean, look at all the people we've met. And if someone's found it, why aren't they telling us?"

Kenny seemed startled by her question at first, but answered, "Do you think someone already has it, and is hiding it from us? From White Crane? Because they want it for themselves?"

"I don't know," said Casey. "But it seems very weird that nobody seems to know about it. What if Journey already has the stick, and just sent us out here on a wild goose chase?"

White Crane started his snowmobile and continued down the ramp. Casey and Kenny looked at each other. "Better follow him," said Casey.

They hopped on their snowmobiles and the group started down the ramp. The sun was at midday, but being fall it would soon be on the southwest horizon. If they were going to get down there and back up before darkness, they would need to hurry.

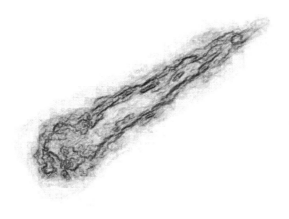

9

Evil Stick

Tyson had joined the group as they descended down into the mine. But why? He was curious; the story was definitely strange, but what if they did find something?

White Crane led the group down the ramp, going faster and faster. He knew too that daylight was precious in the fall, and they would not want to be stuck out in the dark with hungry polar bears around. They needed to find the stick.

As they continued downward, the stranger below was continuing to run around. *Doesn't he get tired?* Kenny thought. As they got closer, White Crane could see that he was not just running around; he seemed to be looking for something. Suddenly White Crane realized that the man had a pole in his hands. A long, black pole.

White Crane stopped and held up his hand to tell the others to stop too. He turned to the three behind him, pointed down below, and said, "That's it, that's the evil polar bear stick."

The group turned and looked below to see the man running with a long black pole in his hands. It was longer than the man was tall. The stick was eight feet, maybe longer.

Kenny turned to White Crane. "I thought you said the polar bear good stick had been found?"

Casey then asked, "I thought the good stick was always found first?"

White Crane was listening, but he was also trying to resolve the situation in his mind. "There is no order to how a stick can be revealed or found. We cannot know for sure this is the only polar bear stick that's been found."

Kenny believed White Crane was right. Maybe the good stick had been found too, and now the evil stick was out. Kenny remembered how much damage Briggs had done when he had the evil owl stick. How the town had been impacted and how his dad had been hurt.

"Kenny," said White Crane, snapping him out his daydream. "We need to locate where he found the stick. We need to know if the good stick is here too."

The group looked at each other, figuring out what they needed to do. "We need a distraction so we can search for the box and the other stick," said Casey.

White Crane agreed. "Kenny, you and Tyson can draw him away with your snowmobiles. Casey and I will search the area."

"What do you want us to do?" asked Kenny.

"Drive your snowmobiles close to him. Let him know you are here," said Casey.

"What if he starts to throw fireballs?" asked Kenny.

"It doesn't look like he has found any rocks," said Casey. "He isn't throwing any. When Briggs found them that was the first thing he did."

"Okay,' said Kenny as he turned to Tyson. "You up for this?"

Tyson looked coldly at Kenny. "So you want me to help you distract this crazy guy so you can find some stick?"

"Yep," said Kenny. "That's the plan."

"Well, then let's have some fun with this guy," said Tyson.

Tyson took off first, driving his snowmobile fast to get down lower so that the crazy man could see them. Kenny followed quickly, but Tyson was good on his snowmobile and left Kenny behind.

Casey and White Crane watched and waited as the two boys made their presence known to the man. Tyson moved in first, very close to the man, then sprayed him with snow to get his attention.

The man reacted and started to chase after Tyson. Kenny caught up and cut off the crazy man, who now saw two guys on snowmobiles cornering him. Tyson and Kenny then started climbing up a small hill of discarded mine rock to draw him away from Casey and White Crane.

The man followed the boys, just as they had planned. Casey and White Crane made their move to begin searching the area.

Tyson was having fun driving his snowmobile around and teasing the crazy man. Kenny followed as they drove up and down the numerous hills of loose rock, taunting the man. The man seemed determined to catch the two boys.

White Crane and Casey snuck down a few more levels and began searching the large mine. Casey watched for openings, areas they could go into. They stopped several times to find caves, but saw no signs of stone boxes, rocks, or any evidence the stick was found here.

Casey decided to voice her concern about the stick. "Do you think the good stick has already been found?"

White Crane looked at Casey. "I do not know if it has been found. But, what are you really asking?"

Casey seemed surprised, and then realized he could tell she was nervous about asking. "Well," she started, "what if one of the villagers already found it and didn't tell us?"

"You're worried Journey lied to us?" he asked.

"Yes. Maybe he doesn't want you to have the stick and is keeping it for himself," said Casey.

"I would not expect him to have any reason to lie to us. He gave me good directions here. He did not send us off a cliff. We are here, the evil stick is here. We are in the right spot. The good polar bear lacrosse stick must be here."

Casey could tell White Crane was not going to be persuaded to believe Journey was lying to him. She decided to keep pushing on the topic to find out what he might be hiding.

"What was the small bag of rocks you gave him?" asked Casey.

White Crane did not seem happy to hear that question. He ignored her question and turned around to start looking again.

But Casey was not going to let him ignore her now. She wanted to know what he was hiding.

"Why wouldn't you talk in front of us last night after dinner?" persisted Casey. "Are you keeping something from us? Something we should know?"

White Crane turned around and with a stern voice said, "Some things, as you say, you do not need to know. If you need to know something I will tell you."

He turned around again and walked away.

Casey looked down the center of the open mine and saw Tyson and Kenny flying around on the snowmobiles. *Well, they seem to be enjoying themselves* she thought. She'd really done it now. She'd upset White Crane and still had no idea where to find the stick.

The chase continued as Kenny checked his gas gauge. He was getting a little low on fuel, and pulled up one more level to stop his snowmobile. Tyson saw Kenny pull up and decided to go over to check on him.

"What's up?" asked Tyson.

"Getting low on fuel," said Kenny. "You see them at all? Have they found anything?"

"I see them over there about 3 rows up from the bottom," said Tyson. "Doesn't look like they have found anything."

Tyson watched as the crazy man moved towards them. "Good thing this guy won't give up! Makes our job easy."

"Yeah, but we need to help them find the stick," said Kenny.

Tyson looked around. "Don't you think he probably found it where they were digging last? I mean the lowest level of the mine?"

Kenny thought for a moment. "Makes sense. Should we tell them to go down there?"

"Na," said Tyson, "we got this. Let's go down and

we can both refuel and find the lowest spot in the mine."

Before Kenny could agree, Tyson started his snowmobile back up and was racing down the hill. Kenny wondered if the crazy man would follow them or find Casey to follow instead.

As soon as Kenny looked up, sure enough the man was following Tyson. Kenny decided to follow Tyson down to the bottom too. Going fast meant they might lose the crazy man, but they needed some time to refuel too.

Kenny pushed his snowmobile faster and faster to catch up to Tyson. Just as Kenny caught up he realized they had reached the lowest level of the mine.

10

Black Stone

Tyson and Kenny got off their snowmobiles and walked around to grab the gas cans to refuel. When Tyson was done he started to look around the area. He knew they would be looking for an area that had fresh dirt, or other signs of recent activity.

"Over here," said Tyson. "This has got to be the spot."

Kenny looked over and saw some smoke coming out of a cave. Not a lot of smoke, but maybe a fire had been burning in there recently. They both grabbed their flashlights and started towards the entrance. The fire pit was right at the entrance of the cave, and Tyson could see it was still hot. Kenny reached out and grabbed Tyson by the shoulder, "Wait, someone could be inside."

Tyson turned to Kenny, saying "There's only one way to find out."

Tyson led the way into the cave, moving slowly, not talking but instead pointing out items to Kenny. A shovel, a pick ax, flashlights, cans of food, and a sleeping bag.

Tyson broke the silence, saying, "Someone has been living here."

Kenny nodded as they split up to look around. The two found various items spread around the cave: a table, chair, some books, lanterns, and a small cook stove.

Kenny found a spot where there was fresh dirt. "Look over here," said Kenny. "Someone was just digging here."

Tyson walked over to see dirt piled up and a large hole on the other side. Tyson saw it. He wasn't sure what it was, but it was black. As he moved closer, he realized it was a very long stone case, almost like a coffin.

"Kenny," said Tyson. "What is this?"

Kenny walked over and examined the large stone container. It was over ten feet long, and was completely black. Just like the evil owl stick container.

The container was open and frighteningly empty, with the lid pushed off onto the ground. Kenny could see polar bear markings of claws, teeth, and eyes. He stood staring at it for a long time. Tyson could see that Kenny was a bit shaken.

Tyson asked, "Kenny, you okay?"

There was no answer as Kenny continued to be lost in thought. "Kenny," he called again. "KENNY!"

Tyson was concerned now. What was going on? Tyson walked over and grabbed Kenny by the arm. Kenny jumped back and looked at Tyson, then back at the container. "You okay?" asked Tyson again.

Kenny nodded. "Yeah, yeah," he said.

"What is this?" asked Tyson.

"It's the evil stick box, the holder of the evil polar bear lacrosse stick," said Kenny.

Tyson bent down and started to inspect the container. The stone was a deep black with markings carved into the stone. The images were polar bear claws, teeth, and eyes, cut in sharp and rough angles. Nothing was smooth, just jagged and angry-looking images. You did not need to know what it was to know it was evil. The person who made this clearly made his point to stay away.

Tyson walked over to the lid on the ground. Similar images were carved there too, and a large red X. "Is that a warning?" asked Tyson.

"I guess," said Kenny. "We saw the same red x on the owl container."

"It looks like a huge coffin," said Tyson.

Kenny remembered thinking the same thing when he found the owl stick. A coffin not meant to be opened.

Kenny mumbled something to himself, but just loud enough for Tyson to hear. "I thought the evil stick was buried below the good stick."

"What was that?" asked Tyson.

Kenny looked over at Tyson. "Just something White Crane told us when we had to find the evil owl lacrosse container. The evil stick was buried below the good stick."

"What does that mean?" asked Tyson.

"We were told to go to the same spot where I found the good owl lacrosse stick, then look below it. It would always be buried below the good stick."

"What happened?" asked Tyson.

"We went back to the spot where I had found the owl stick. We couldn't find it, but we heard someone else below us. When we reached the lower level Briggs had already found it. He ran out of the mine before we could stop him."

"Then?' asked Tyson, who wanted to know more of the story.

"He went crazy, running around like our guy outside. But he found the rocks that shot fireballs and started to hurt people," Kenny paused. "He hurt my dad pretty bad."

Tyson could see Kenny did not want to continue the story. Painful memories. But Tyson needed to know. He asked, "So what happened to Briggs?"

"I was told I had to kill him," said Kenny. "But I couldn't. I wouldn't. Then, after he hurt my dad, I started to get angry. White Crane, Casey, and others helped me take the evil stick away from Briggs."

"Was Briggs okay?" asked Tyson.

"Yeah, once we got it away from him, and with some time he recovered," said Kenny.

"Why were you told to kill him?" asked Tyson.

"The good stick bonds to the person who finds it

first. It stays bonded to that person until they die. Then it is passed on to the next person who touches it. We all assumed the evil stick worked the same way. But it didn't. Once Briggs lost the stick he quit acting crazy and calmed down."

"Where is the evil owl stick now?" asked Tyson.

"White Crane took it and hid it," said Kenny. "I assume he wants to do the same here. But we need to find the good polar bear lacrosse stick."

"You said the evil stick was always buried lower than the good stick," said Tyson.

"Yeah, so we must go up a level in the mine," said Kenny as he lifted his left hand and pointed up.

Tyson's eyes followed Kenny's hand as it pointed up and saw something in the rock above Kenny's head.

"There it is!" exclaimed Tyson.

Sure enough, as Kenny looked up to where he was pointing, he saw a white container. It was only partially exposed but Kenny and Tyson could see the markings.

"We need to dig it out," said Tyson. Kenny realized that with all the excitement, Tyson was now starting to believe their story. The Flamethrowers story.

The ceiling of the cave was pretty high and they could not reach it from the ground. They could see where someone had started digging at the ceiling but had stopped.

"Let's grab the table to stand on, and get the shovel and pick ax," said Kenny.

After climbing onto the table, the boys started to dig away at the area around the white container. It wasn't easy, though. The angle was tough, and the table was not very stable. They took turns chopping at the dirt in the ceiling while the table moved and shook with each swing.

While swinging away, Kenny thought that his mom would probably not approve of the situation. Here were two teenage boys standing on a shaky table, one swinging a pick ax, the other swinging a shovel. He was glad his mom was not there.

The digging went on and they began to tire. The ground was hard and the dirt was falling onto their heads and into their eyes.

Finally Kenny stopped, and got down off the table. He held the table steady while Tyson kept swinging away. Kenny was tired and they had not made much progress. As Kenny was leaning against the table, Tyson slipped while swinging the pick ax.

"LOOK OUT!" he yelled to Kenny.

Kenny backed up as the pick ax missed his head, but did catch his arm, tearing his jacket and cutting a small gash in his arm.

"Whoa!" shouted Kenny.

Tyson jumped down off the table.

"Sorry Kenny, lost my footing."

"It's okay," said Kenny. "Just a small cut. We need to get some help or try something else. I'm exhausted."

They sat down to catch their breath. While they rested, Tyson wanted to know more about the story.

"Why are these lacrosse sticks buried?" asked Tyson.

"That's a much longer story, and better told by White Crane," said Kenny. "Let's just say there was a big fight and the Creator took the sticks away from the Nations."

"I should ask the obvious question. What is lacrosse?" asked Tyson.

Kenny smiled and said, "I hadn't known before this summer either. I saw kids playing it in a park. They were visiting from the Twin Cities to attend my brother's hockey camp. White Crane told us stories about how the sport started as a healing game and entertainment for the Creator. It's actually a fun game, with a ball you pick up with your lacrosse stick and try to score by putting it in the goal. White Crane has told us stories about large games between nations, and everyone could play."

Tyson was sure there was more to learn about lacrosse, but he wanted that container too.

"Okay, well we better go get Casey and White Crane," said Tyson. "We need to show them what we found."

Meanwhile, up a few levels, Casey and White Crane came out of a small cave they had been searching. Casey couldn't hear the sound of snowmobiles anymore. She said, "Something's wrong."

White Crane looked around and could not see anyone. "You're right. Where are the boys? The man?"

Suddenly the crazy man appeared in front of them. He wasn't running as before. His eyes! Casey noticed his eyes. They were orange and red with the color bouncing around like fire. White Crane instinctively pushed Casey behind him. His stick was in the snowmobile, and that was not close to them now.

The man did not move. He studied them, trying to make sense of these people and why they were there. The three stood silent and White Crane stayed between Casey and the man. Casey could see the polar bear stick in his hands. The stick was long, much longer than the man was tall. The fur at the top was pitch black.

Then a voice could be heard from below. "Casey! Where are you?"

11

Fireball

Tyson and Kenny walked out of the cave, yelling for White Crane and Casey. As they looked around, they could not see them or their snowmobiles.

Casey and White Crane were defenseless and did not want to provoke the man standing in front of them, so they did not answer Kenny and Tyson.

The man realized that the boys were calling from down below and walked over to the edge of the ramp. Seeing Kenny and Tyson off their snowmobiles and wandering around his camp, he started running towards them.

Kenny and Tyson had their backs turned to the spot where the man was running down the hill. They did not see him at first. Casey ran to the edge and yelled down, "Kenny, he's coming!"

Tyson and Kenny heard her and looked up to see Casey first, then the man running towards them. Kenny ran towards his snowmobile but the man was closing fast. Instead of starting it, he grabbed his backpack and lacrosse stick and ran into the cave.

Tyson, seeing Kenny run into the cave, followed. The lanterns they lit earlier were still glowing as Kenny and Tyson ran back to the black stone container. Kenny realized now that maybe he should have stayed outside. They were trapped and the man was standing at the only exit.

Kenny and Tyson watched as the man slowly entered. No crazy motions anymore. No crazy yelling or waving the long stick. Instead, he was calm. Just calm, and watching them. Tyson looked at the man's eyes. "Kenny, what's with his eyes?"

Kenny noticed too. They were orange and red, dancing like there was a fire going on behind the eyes. Kenny shook his head.

The man did not move any closer, but stood and watched, like he was thinking about his next move and unsure who these boys were.

"What should we do?" asked Tyson.

Kenny answered, "We need to get out of here. We need to move him back."

With that Kenny put down his backpack and opened it. He grabbed a rock and placed it in the pouch of his lacrosse stick. It started glowing, just like he showed Koti the night before. Tyson watched as the rock got brighter and brighter. But before it could catch fire Kenny shot the rock right at the feet of the man blocking their path.

Whammm! There was a small explosion and the man fell backwards onto the ground. The explosion had surprised the man; he did not understand what had just happened. The man grunted as he tried to roll over and get onto his feet.

Tyson started to walk slowly towards the man. There was something familiar now. That voice. *Could it be?*

Tyson felt a little faint. He was feeling confusion, dread, anger, hope. *Could it be?*

Tyson stopped advancing and shined his flashlight

directly on the man's face. The unshaved face with ratty hair was squinting back. Softly Tyson asked, "Dad?"

"What?" cried out Kenny.

"Dad!" exclaimed Tyson. "It's my dad!"

Kenny was trying to process what he'd just heard. What was Tyson talking about? Why would his dad be living here in the mine? This made no sense. But Tyson seemed sure.

As the man stayed on the ground, Tyson started approaching him closer.

"Stay back," warned Kenny.

Tyson ignored him. He was trying to figure out what was going on. He had thought his dad was gone. And all this time his dad had been living in this mine. The place he visited almost every month to remind him of what he had lost.

Tyson needed to know. He needed to be sure.

"Dad," said Tyson. "Is that you? What is going on? Why have you been living here?"

Kenny kept a close eye on the man. If he moved, he would grab Tyson and pull him back.

But there was no answer from the man. Tyson took another step, causing the man to flinch. Kenny pulled Tyson back a couple of steps. The man sat up, holding the stick. He looked at the boys. Slowly he began to get up. Tyson was sure it was his dad now. *But why is he here and with that stick?*

"Dad," said Tyson. "What's going on?"

Kenny could hear Tyson pleading with his dad to talk with him. But he wasn't sure what to expect. *Will he attack us? Will he give his son a hug? Does he recognize Tyson?*

Kenny began to realize that even if this was his dad, it was not the dad Tyson remembered. He had the evil stick and just like Briggs, he was not going to care who got in his way.

"Tyson," said Kenny. "I know it's your dad, but it's NOT YOUR DAD! He has the evil stick and we cannot reason with him. He will hurt you."

"Shut up Kenny," said Tyson. "This is not your concern. It's my dad. He needs my help."

Tyson continued pleading with his dad to answer him. But the man just stared back. Tyson continued taking slow steps towards the man. Tyson was close enough now to see the detail of polar bear stick. *Wow, this is what was in that black stone box? This is so creepy, and very real. The detail of the polar bears carved on the shaft of the stick is amazing.*

Tyson reached out and asked, "Dad, can I touch

it?"

After yelling down to Kenny, Casey leapt onto her snowmobile and started down the mine. White Crane was right behind her. Casey could see that Kenny had not gotten back onto the snowmobile, so he must have run away from the man somewhere.

Casey rode down as fast as see could. Suddenly she heard an explosion. She looked around and saw smoke coming out of an area near Kenny's snowmobile. Casey pushed the snowmobile even faster.

12

Tyson out

Before Kenny realized what was happening, the man's eyes opened wide and the fire in them grew bright.

Kenny called out, "No!"

But it was too late.

The man pulled the stick away from Tyson's reach and swung the stick at Tyson's head. Kenny reacted to stop the blow with his stick, but the owl stick was no match for the polar bear stick. Kenny only slowed the blow to Tyson's head.

Kenny's stick went flying out of his hands, while Tyson collapsed to the ground.

Kenny realized he had to have his stick and raced to pick it up just in time to stop a second blow.

Dazed, Kenny scrambled deeper into the cave and saw his backpack. He grabbed a rock from the backpack and moved back, giving it time to heat up. He did not send a warning shot but went right at the man.

This time, however, the man was ready, and used his lacrosse stick to deflect the flaming rock away from him. Kenny realized he was in trouble. The polar bear stick was powerful and Kenny was not going to be able to defeat him alone.

Kenny scrambled around the cave, trying to get around the man. He leapt up on ledges, trying to get to higher ground. But the polar bear stick just crushed the fireballs that Kenny threw.

Kenny knew he just had to buy some time until Casey and White Crane arrived to help. *What is taking them so long?*

Kenny saw a chance to reach his backpack again and spilled the bag open. That would let him keep moving and scoop balls up as needed to shoot them.

As soon as he thought his great plan was going to help him, he realized the man could also scoop a ball. Quickly Kenny loaded a ball and shot it. But just as quickly as he shot it, it was deflected.

The man saw a chance to scoop up a rock. As he tried to lift his stick, Kenny slashed him in the leg. Stumbling down from Kenny's blow, the man staggered away.

Kenny saw his chance to start loading up on shots. He scooped the next ball and took a hard shot right at the man's head. Again the polar bear stick deflected Kenny's shot. However, the shot had been hard enough that it knocked the man backwards a few steps. Kenny shot again, pushing him back a few more feet.

Okay I can push him back, thought Kenny. *I need to keep going.* Kenny scooped rock after rock and kept throwing them at the man. Sometimes in his hurry Kenny even shot regular rocks not realizing in the darkness that they wouldn't become fireballs.

Casey and White Crane arrived and ran towards the cave. They could hear a lot of explosions now and they knew Kenny was fighting hard. Casey saw the man backing out of the cave because he was getting hit by Kenny's fireballs.

She backed up and turned to White Crane, who was pulling his own stick out of his pack. She yelled out to Kenny, "We're here, Kenny!"

Kenny heard Casey's voice but was afraid to stop shooting.

White Crane pulled out his white lacrosse stick. Casey watched as the stick seemed to become a part of him. White Crane loaded a single rock from his sack and started to walk towards the entrance. He would only need one rock.

Kenny was getting low on rocks and began to slow down, but he had done his job. The man and stick were out of the cave.

The man was now exposed outside. He saw Casey and then White Crane walking towards him. He saw White Crane had a stick and it was on fire. White Crane held it for a long time as the fireball grew very large.

The man realized that Kenny had stopped shooting and turned his full attention to White Crane. Casey watched as White Crane made a quick shot directly at the left foot of the man. The man tried to jump up to miss the throw, which hit directly below his left foot. The explosion sent him high into the air.

Casey watched as the man landed some two levels above them. The man was clearly shaken and hurt.

"That was some shot," admired Casey.

White Crane turned and smiled at Casey. "Let's get Kenny."

Kenny felt the blast of the explosion but did not see the man get hit. The entrance was now covered in debris, so Kenny went to cover his new friend to protect him. Casey ran into the cave and found Kenny leaning over Tyson, who was unconscious on the ground. Kenny and Tyson were covered in dirt from the earlier digging and more recent explosions. Casey only recognized Kenny from his eyes, which were the only clean thing about him.

White Crane stayed outside at first to watch the man as he got up. The man, seeing there were now two Flamethrowers to challenge him, and that he had no fireballs to throw, seemed to decide to retreat and fight another time.

As the man moved farther up the mine, White Crane entered the cave.

"What happened to young Tyson?" asked White

Crane.

"He was knocked out by the polar bear stick," said Kenny. "I tried to stop it, but I only managed to soften the blow."

White Crane knelt beside Tyson to check that he was breathing. "He is lucky to be alive," said White Crane.

"There's another thing," said Kenny. "He thinks the man with the polar bear stick is his dad."

Casey looked puzzled. They didn't know much about him. They had just met him that day. She turned to look at White Crane.

White Crane did not seem concerned or surprised by the news. Casey was wondering what was up now. *How much does White Crane know that he hasn't shared?*

"Doesn't it seem strange we just meet a kid, and it's his dad who found the polar bear stick?" asked Casey.

"We are here for a purpose," said White Crane. "We cannot be certain of our role. We all have a role to play. We must help each other. Right now Tyson needs our help."

"It's gonna be dark soon," said Casey.

"Yes, we will need to get him home," said White

Crane.

Kenny walked over to pick up his backpack, which was basically empty from all the shooting he was doing. As he turned around, he remembered what he and Tyson were doing before the man had shown up.

"Wait!" cried out Kenny, pointing upwards. "We found the stone container! Look!"

Casey and White Crane walked over to the large tomb-like box.

"Wow," said Casey as she touched the black surface, feeling its rough edges. "It's huge!"

"Must be over 10 feet long," said Kenny.

White Crane took a great interest in the container as well. He examined it closely, as if he was looking for something.

"What do you think?" asked Casey. "Just like the owl containers?"

White Crane continued to study it, looking at each portion of the lid and the inside and outside of the box.

"We also found the polar bear good stick," said Kenny, as he pointed to the ceiling of the cave.

Casey bolted up and stared at the white box sticking out the rocks above her.

"Cool," said Casey. "We found it...you found it."

White Crane looked excited. "Nice job, Kenny."

He then walked over to where Tyson was. "We need to get him home," he said.

"White Crane, sir, we can get the polar bear stick now!" said Kenny. "Then we can match his power when we face him again."

Casey started to get excited too. She realized she would be the one to get the stick. Tyson was hurt and she would get the opportunity to get a Flamethrower stick.

Kenny was thinking the same thing, "We can have Casey get the stick. It won't take long to get it down."

White Crane turned to the kids and looked back up at the white box. He said, "We must get Tyson home. We need to help him. We can get the stick later. No one else knows it's here."

"He does," said Kenny pointing outside the cave. "That man does, and what happens if he opens it?"

Casey thought, *wow that is a good question. What would happen? Could a single person have both sticks at once and the power from both?*

"We have time to get Tyson home," said White Crane. "Besides, the stick is not for Casey."

Kenny and Casey looked at each other.

"We are the only ones who made this trip out here," said Kenny. "Who else do you think would get it?"

Casey was trying to think what else White Crane knew the he was not sharing. Did he know Tyson would be here? Could he have been promised the stick last night when Journey talked to White Crane? Who really was going to get this stick? But then she also remembered that when they came to the mine they assumed the good stick had been already found. So she had not even expected that a stick was available for her.

Yet, there it was, sticking out of the ceiling. An unclaimed Flamethrower lacrosse stick, just feet away.

Kenny and Casey struggled to make sense of White Crane's demand that Casey not get the stick.

"Why did you bring us here?" asked Kenny, now getting some anger in his voice. "You said everyone has a role. Maybe this is Casey's role, the polar bear Flamethrower?"

"Tyson is meant for this stick," White Crane said firmly. "There is no debate."

Kenny could feel his anger growing and Casey

109

knew this was not going to do any good. They could talk later; she needed to defuse the situation. She walked over to Kenny and grabbed his arm and said, "It's okay Kenny, we need to get Tyson help. The stick will be here when we come back." She turned her eyes to White Crane. Looking directly at him, she added, "Right? It will be here when we come back?"

White Crane nodded in agreement. She made sure he knew they were all coming back for the stick.

Kenny could feel his racing heart start to slow down. He always trusted Casey. They had been through a lot together and she was the calm one. *Trust her,* he put in his mind, *trust her.*

The group worked together to load Tyson onto the back of White Crane's snowmobile. They had blankets and packed him in nice and warm.

Kenny loaded his mostly-empty backpack of rocks onto his snowmobile. He looked around as he climbed aboard. *There must be more rocks around here. And what if Tyson's dad finds them first?*

Kenny started his snowmobile. He was still mad at White Crane for not letting Casey get the stick. Maybe Casey was right, maybe Journey was influencing White Crane. But White Crane had been

110

so helpful in the past. What would be his reason for keeping them in the dark? So many questions for the long ride back.

As they came over a ridge the village lights could be seen. White Crane stopped his snowmobile and got off.

"I am low on fuel, and we did not fill up before we left the mine. Can you refuel and I will check on Tyson?" asked White Crane.

Kenny got off and started to refuel White Crane's snowmobile and then walked over to Casey.

"Use some fuel too?" asked Kenny.

"Yes," answered Casey.

"How does Tyson look?" asked Casey.

"Not sure, White Crane is checking on him," answered Kenny.

"You okay?" asked Casey.

"Not really," he said.

"We can talk when we get back," she said.

"Okay, I better check on Tyson too," said Kenny.

Kenny walked to the sled that held Tyson.

"How's he doing?" asked Kenny.

"He's cold, but he's moving and groaning, so he's conscious. Need to get going, get him some shelter,"

111

said White Crane.

As Kenny walked back to his snowmobile, he saw three polar bears walking on the same ridge. He could tell they were watching. Kenny wondered if they could tell that Tyson was hurt.

No free dinner tonight boys. The group headed towards the lights.

13

Home Again

The sky was completely dark now. White Crane led the group to a very small cabin. Casey had turned to Kenny as if to say, *what are we doing? This is not the place we left from?*

White Crane brought his snowmobile to a stop. He got off and before he could walk towards the cabin a woman came running out.

"Tyson," she cried. "Where is Tyson?"

White Crane pointed to the sled on the back of his snowmobile. She ran to his side while Kenny and Casey watched.

Casey wondered, *How did he know where to go?*

"What happened?" asked Yuraa. "Was he attacked again?"

"Let's get him inside," said White Crane.

The four of them helped lift Tyson and carried him into the house. Inside it was warm, with a pipe stove in the center of the room. They laid Tyson on the couch and his mom put blankets on him. She then heated some water for tea.

"You are not from our village," said Tyson's mom.

"No," said White Crane. "We are from another place, Minnesota."

"I see," said the mom. "What happened to my son?"

As she began to ask questions, Tyson sat up.

"Mom," said Tyson. "I'm okay."

She ran over to look at her son.

Tyson continued, "Kenny here saved me."

Kenny smiled.

She glanced at Kenny, but kept her attention on

her son.

"Are you sure you're okay?" asked mom.

"Yes," said Tyson. "But my head hurts, bad."

Tyson laid his head back down on the couch. Sitting up was causing him too much pain.

"What happened?" asked his mom again.

"Well…" started Tyson, "Dad's alive."

With those words spoken, Tyson closed his eyes and passed out. His mom wasn't sure she heard him right. Besides, he seemed delirious.

But she asked the others, "What does he mean? His dad is alive?"

Casey responded, "He thinks a person we met today is his father."

"Can't be," said the mom. "He disappeared years ago. No one has seen or heard from him since. What did he look like? Did you talk with him?" she asked.

"Well," said Casey. "We didn't really get a chance to talk."

Kenny chimed in, "After he hit Tyson we really didn't hang around for a conversation."

"His father did this to them?" she asked in more confusion.

The conversation was not going well. White Crane, holding up his hands, tried to quiet everyone down. A knock came at the door.

"Who's that?" asked Kenny.

Tyson's mom went to the door. It was cold out and two figures stood in the doorway covered in fur. Even covered up she knew who it was.

"Come in Journey, Koti," she said. "Why are you here?"

Journey glanced at White Crane and then at the others around the room. He then said, "We heard you were back. You did not come back to the cottage."

"We needed to return a wounded son to his mother," said White Crane.

Casey and Kenny could feel the tension in their voices. Journey was clearly unhappy about White Crane not coming to see him first.

"Is everything okay?" asked Journey. "How is Tyson doing?"

No one seemed willing to answer at first. Kenny and Casey could feel the stress building between Journey and White Crane, and they did not want to get in the middle of it. Tyson's mom finally said, "He is in and out. He is not making sense. Talked about finding Blade, his father."

Journey turned to White Crane, "Is this true? Did

he find his father after all these years?"

"Tyson seemed to think so," said White Crane. "But who am I to judge? I did not know the man."

"No," said Journey. "No you did not."

"We should take him to the clinic," said his mom.

"No," said Journey, "we should not move him. He has been through enough today. We will get the doctor to come here."

Koti walked over and knelt by Tyson. He looked at his head and could see where Tyson took the blow. A large lump had formed just above the right side of his hairline. *No bleeding, that is good* he thought. He and Tyson attended school together and Koti knew Tyson was prone to rages and wanderings, looking for his father.

Koti turned to Casey and asked, "Where did you find him?"

"He was at the mine when we arrived," said Casey. "He was already there."

Journey motioned to White Crane and the two of them slipped away to another room. Casey noticed the two moving away even as Koti continued to talk with her.

"Do you think it was his father?" asked Koti.

Kenny answered, "He was convinced it was his

dad. He wanted to help him. We saw evidence that this guy, whoever he was, had been living there for quite some time."

"What makes you think that?" asked Casey.

Casey had been on the outside and had not talked to Kenny yet about all the stuff that went on before she and White Crane got down to them. So she was curious too.

"We found food, lanterns, table, chair, sleeping bag. Just stuff that made us think someone had been living there for a while."

"Did you talk to the father?" asked Koti, looking at Kenny.

"No he was not in a mood for talking," said Kenny.

"He means that the guy found the evil polar bear stick and was acting crazy, trying to hurt us," said Casey.

"Whoa," said Koti. "Really? He found the polar bear stick? How?"

Casey's attention had moved back to White Crane and Journey. She could see them talking and Journey was looking very upset by the conversation. White Crane remained calm but Casey could tell he was struggling. It had been a long trip and he was tired and frustrated with whatever Journey was arguing about.

Tyson's mom spoke up after hearing about the polar bear stick. "What are you talking about? What is a polar bear stick?"

Her voice was not soft, and her question got the attention of White Crane and Journey. They walked over to talk with her.

Journey, who was the elder of the village and their storyteller, than began to tell a version of the Flamethrowers to her. Kenny, Casey, and the others all listened as Journey told the story of the Creator and the game now called lacrosse. About the Flamethrowers, who were teachers and guardians of the game. About the betrayal, due to jealousy, by a man who murdered for unjust reasons. The loss of Flamethrower sticks as they were buried until such a day that they would be returned for a better purpose.

Tyson's mom was sitting on the couch, holding her son's hand. She was hearing the story but it made no sense to her. She was there in the moment with no husband, an injured son, and some people who brought her son home injured.

Tyson opened his eyes again. He was surrounded by people. His eyesight was blurry but he could feel his mother's hand.

"Mom," he said. "I'm thirsty."

Koti motioned to her to stay on the couch with her son, and went to get some water. Tyson wanted to sit up but the whole group seemed to hold him down.

"You need to stay down," said his mom. "You passed out last time you sat up."

Tyson stayed down while Koti brought the water. He took a few sips and then started talking. "Dad. I found Dad."

Mom was still skeptical. "Your friends say you found someone. But I don't think –"

Tyson interrupted, "I know. I know he is my dad." Tyson paused and remembered why he recognized him. "The bandana! He had Osseo's bandana around his neck. You know he carried that everywhere, after…" Tyson's voice trailed off. He did not want to remind his mother of the death of her other son, Osseo.

"You saw the bandana?" asked his mom. "You sure?"

"Yes," said Tyson softly, "it had the stains."

Tyson was referring to the blood stains that were left on the bandana. After Osseo had died, his father kept the bandana and never took it off. A reminder of the son he had lost. But it was that same bandana he saw every day that reminded him of his lost brother and a father who could not, would not forgive himself.

Tyson's mom began to cry, and then her tears turned to determination. "I am going to the mine tomorrow to find my husband," she said.

White Crane and the others were not expecting Yurra to want to get involved. They had their own plans of going back and getting the stick.

Journey said, "I do not think it wise. You should not go and see him like this."

"See him like what?" she asked.

"He is possessed by the evil side of the stick," said Journey. "We do not know what is going to happen to him."

"Happen to him!" she said. "Happen to him! I will tell you what is going to happen to him! We are going to bring him back."

Tyson was excited now to see that his mother believed him. He echoed her words. "Yes, we are going to bring my father home."

Journey pleaded, "He is not himself Tyson. You going back will only make it worse."

White Crane quickly responded, "Tyson you can go with us, but your mother must stay home."

Journey leered at White Crane. "Koti can go with you tomorrow. Tyson was hurt and does not need to risk more injuries."

As Kenny and Casey listened, it started to become obvious that Journey did not want Tyson to go back to the mine. That meant only one thing to Casey: Journey wanted his son to get the stick, not Tyson. That was the real argument, but Journey didn't want to say that in front of Tyson's mother.

"This is not the time to discuss this," said White Crane. "Let us all rest and we can make plans in the morning."

Journey and Koti began to leave. "We shall see you in the morning."

14

Her Way

Kenny woke up and heard discussions going on in the kitchen. Tyson was talking with White Crane, but Kenny was still rubbing the sleep from his eyes and not listening. Kenny saw Tyson's mom packing items for the trip. Casey was eating at the table when Kenny walked into the room.

"Your mom needs to stay home," White Crane urged Tyson.

"Well good luck trying to talk my mom into doing something," said Tyson. Tyson knew these last few years were tough on his mom, doing things alone. He knew his mom would do anything she put her mind to, and she taught him the same. She would tell Tyson *this land is no place for the soft; to survive, you must be tough and never give up.*

White Crane could sense he was losing the argument. This mother and son had developed a strong bond that he was not going to break. She was going along and Tyson, regardless of how his head felt, was not going to let his mother go alone.

White Crane had been through many tough times too. He was not about to give up so quickly.

The sound of approaching snowmobiles could be heard. Journey and his son were approaching from the east. Inside, the group continued to pack and get ready for the return trip to the diamond mine.

Journey and Koti pulled up to the house, where White Crane stood outside, waiting for them.

"Yuraa is insisting on going," said White Crane.

"We need to help her understand that this person is not who she thinks he is."

"I agree. They both should stay home," said Journey.

White Crane wanted Tyson to get the Flamethrower stick, while Journey wanted his son,

Koti, to receive it.

White Crane wanted help convincing Yuraa to stay home, so he asked Journey for help. "Will you speak with her?" asked White Crane. "Keep her safe, keep her here. You know what could happen."

"Of course, but you know what I want," said Journey.

"The stick belongs to Tyson," said White Crane.

"How do you know this?" demanded Journey. "You come here from the States, to our village, and you get to decide who should be the Flamethrower here?"

White Crane knew this was going to be a tough sell. Journey had a point: who was he, an elder from another village, just like him, to decide that fate. But he knew something Journey didn't. And he was not ready to share this with anyone.

Journey continued, "And who is this Kenny and Casey to you? Why are they here? Why is Kenny a Flamethrower?"

"Kenny found the owl stick before I met him," said White Crane. "He was chosen for this. The Creator works in mysterious ways."

"It isn't right," said Journey. "And it's my son's right to have the polar bear stick. It belongs to our village."

"Tyson is from your village," said White Crane.

"Perhaps, but he is not from the chief's clan, like my son," said Journey.

White Crane was frustrated at the back and forth and it was getting him no closer to keeping Tyson's mom home.

"Will you please speak to her?" asked White Crane again.

Journey knew his best chance to get his son the stick was to convince both mother and son to not go today. Journey entered the house and saw Yuraa in the kitchen preparing some food to bring on the trip.

As Journey entered the kitchen, Yuraa did not look up and simply said, "You can save your breath old man, I will be going to bring my husband home today."

Journey was ready for her objection, "It would be best if Tyson does not go today. He has been hurt and needs to recover."

His comments caught Yuraa off guard. She had expected him to fight her going. Now he was using her son as an excuse for her not to go.

"Tyson has seen his father. I doubt any of us could keep him away," said Yuraa.

"He is weak and could be injured again with another encounter with his father," said Journey, trying to find some way to convince her to make Tyson stay.

"Tyson!" called out his mother, causing everyone to startle. "Come in here."

Journey was feeling nervous now. He knew Tyson would not appreciate his efforts to keep him home.

"Journey feels you are too injured to travel today," she said.

Tyson turned to face Journey.

"What say you?" she continued defiantly.

"The elder should not be concerned about me," said Tyson. "We are both going."

Journey tried to speak again but Yuraa held up the knife that was in her hand. "Do not speak to me again today!" she said. "After the tragedies, you did not reach out to us. You did not care to know how we were doing, if we had food enough. You were not worrying or caring about us until yesterday. I have not seen you in my home for years, and yet in the past two days you have been here telling me what not to do. My son and I have a duty to his father. We will do what we have to, so he can return to us."

Tyson's posture changed, standing taller than he ever had. His mother believed in him and was standing up to Journey. *Yes, we are going to get my father home* he thought.

Tyson walked over to Journey to show him the way out of his home. Tyson said nothing; he knew he didn't have to. His mom had spoken.

Journey turned and looked at his son in the other room, who was speaking with Kenny and Casey. "Time for us to go," Journey said.

Koti started walking towards the door and Kenny and Casey began to follow.

Journey held out his hand to Kenny and Casey. "Stay here, for now."

Kenny and Casey stopped and looked over to Tyson. "Let them go," said Tyson.

White Crane was still outside when Journey and Koti came out of the house. "She is your problem," said Journey. "I cannot stop her."

Journey walked away from White Crane and towards his snowmobile. Koti was confused and asked his father, "Where are you going? I thought we were going with them? To help them?"

"It is not our trek to make today," said Journey. "White Crane shall lead them, not us."

"Father, I don't understand," said Koti. "They need our help. We can help bring the father home."

Journey reached his snowmobile and lifted a large sack and handed it to his son. White Crane watched as Koti lifted the heavy sack and started to walk towards him.

Kenny, Casey, and Tyson walked out of the house and watched White Crane and Journey, trying to understand what was going on.

"What is he doing?" Kenny asked Casey.

Koti slowly walked towards the group, with a large grey sack over his shoulder. It must have been heavy because Koti, a strong young man, was struggling to walk in a straight line.

As Koti reached the group, he dropped the sack at White Crane's feet. "My father asked me to give these to you."

"Thank you, Koti," said White Crane.

As Koti turned to walk away Casey asked, "Aren't you going with us?"

Koti answered, "My father does not want me to go with you. He is not happy with the path White Crane has chosen."

"What's in the sack?" asked Tyson.

"Fire rocks," answered Koti. He then turned to

White Crane, saying, "My father made them as you instructed."

Koti then reached into his jacket pocket and brought out a small black bag. It was the same bag that Kenny and Casey had seen White Crane give Journey when they arrived.

"You can make the fireballs?" asked Kenny.

White Crane did not answer and Koti turned and walked back to his father. White Crane knew this division between villages was a bad omen on their quest. Still, White Crane believed he was doing the right thing with Tyson, and Journey was free to accept the decision or not.

Casey and Kenny started to talk about the fireballs. White Crane knew they were curious but now was not the time to distract them further. They would be facing a powerful force soon, and their focus needed to be on that.

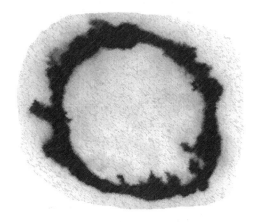

15

Ridge of Fire

Yuraa came out of the house suited up and ready to go. She loaded items onto her snowmobile and took off. Tyson followed closely behind.

White Crane gestured to Kenny and Casey to load the large grey sack that Koti had dropped off, and in a few minutes they were on their way too.

White Crane was uneasy. Yuraa did not wait for the others and had simply left on her own. This was not a good sign to start the day.

Tyson had caught up to his mom and took the lead. He didn't know if she really knew the way or not. He knew exactly where to enter the mine when they got there, and wanted to lead the way. But it was hard to keep up with her.

Casey was worried that Koti was not coming along. She knew his father was stopping him, but she did not know why. She was also distracted by the polar bear stick. She wondered if maybe Tyson wouldn't want it and she could get it. White Crane and Kenny already had a stick, and maybe she could get a Flamethrower stick today.

She knew White Crane had prevented her before, but this was a new adventure, and maybe he would change his mind. Plus, Kenny was on her side. He wanted her to have it. Maybe, she thought, she even deserved to get one, having gone all this way with them.

Casey's mind wandered off, and she watched the caribou move away from them. Suddenly Casey saw Kenny veer hard left. She could not see why at first, but quickly did the same. A large polar bear had blocked their path, and was standing on his hind legs. He towered over them.

Kenny looked back to see if Casey was okay, then looked forward again to see a faint view of two snowmobiles in front of him. *Almost caught up to them* he thought. Tyson and his mom were within view. Kenny sped up again to try to catch up before they reached the mine.

Tyson arrived at the edge of the mine first, showing his mom where the trail into the mine began. Tyson was still pointing when Kenny, Casey, and White Crane arrived just moments later.

White Crane pulled in front of all the others, then turned off his machine.

"What's the plan?" asked Casey.

White Crane liked her excitement but he knew she was the least of his worries right now. He focused his attention on Tyson.

"Kenny and I will draw your dad's attention. Casey and your mom will help you get the stick."

"His name is Blade," said the mother, "and I will go with you to meet my husband."

Tyson chimed in too. "You are not going to hurt my dad. Maybe I should go to him first."

This was exactly why White Crane hadn't wanted Yuraa to come along. She and Tyson were focusing on the wrong challenge.

"We must first get the good polar bear lacrosse stick," White Crane insisted. "We cannot defeat the evil without it."

"See, you do want to hurt my dad, just like before," said Tyson.

Kenny saw how angry Tyson was.

"We can help your dad once we have the good stick. We cannot match his power without it," added Kenny.

"Casey, stay close to Tyson and help him get the stick out," said White Crane, his back to the mine entrance.

"Incoming!" yelled Kenny, as he knocked Tyson down and started running towards Casey.

Casey saw the fireball and it was closing fast. They, on the other hand, were slow-moving in the snow. Her boots felt like they weighed a ton.

The fireball landed right in front of her, sending her flying back into a bank of snow. Kenny quickly got to her. Casey was dazed, but Kenny did not see any injuries.

"Casey! You okay?" asked Kenny.

Casey moaned for a moment and opened her eyes. Things were blurry and she was a bit confused about where she was.

"Here comes another," shouted Tyson.

The fireball went past the group as they ducked down.

"Where is that coming from?" asked Yuraa.

"He's found the fireballs," said Kenny.

"Who?" asked Yuraa.

"Blade," said White Crane.

"My husband is shooting fire at us...?" asked Yuraa in confusion. "No, this does not make sense."

"Mom," said Tyson. "It's true he has the polar bear evil stick and attacked me before. We need to be careful. We need to help him."

Yuraa was struggling to understand. She did not want to listen about good and evil sticks. *These were just White Crane's stories*, she told herself. She was here to see her husband. She had to see him before believing that he could possibly be hurling fire at her and their son.

Kenny stayed by Casey's side as the fireballs continued to go by. The man could not really see them; he was just trying to scare them.

As Casey gained her wits about her, she looked at White Crane. "What if Tyson goes with you to help his father and I can get the polar bear stick?"

Why does everyone want this stick? wondered White

135

Crane. *Do they not see the jealousy this has already caused?*

White Crane's frustration became obvious as he answered her directly. "The stick is not yours to have, Casey! It is not your job to be a Flamethrower!"

Casey was surprised and upset by White Crane's response. She sat up and snapped back, "FINE!"

She turned to Tyson and said, "Let's go get your stick."

Kenny helped her up. Just as he did, they saw Yuraa start her snowmobile and start down the ramp into the mine.

"NO!" yelled White Crane.

But it was too late; Yuraa had decided that she must see her husband first, before listening to any more stories. So she left, alone.

Yuraa sped off down the hill and out of sight.

"Mom!" yelled Tyson. "Nooooo…" he cried out, his voice trailing off, watching his mother leave him.

The others felt uncomfortable, not sure what to say to Tyson. Casey reached out to touch Tyson's arm, but the group remained silent. After a few moments, Kenny decided to refocus them.

"Casey, are you ready to go?" asked Kenny.

"I can't believe she just took off," said Casey.

The group stared for a moment as she left them at the top of the ridge. She was ahead of them and they would not be able to catch her on the snowmobiles. White Crane was going to have to break the mood.

He realized that he needed to fly down to reach her in time.

"Kenny, the only way we can stop her is to fly directly down," said White Crane.

"Kenny hasn't learned to fly yet," said Casey, with alarm in her voice.

"Yeah," said Kenny. "It's been on my list but I haven't had --."

White Crane cut him off, "No time like the present to learn a new skill."

"You can fly?" asked Tyson.

"Well, it's like we said before, you can get the abilities of the animal your lacrosse stick was made from," said Kenny. Kenny turned to White Crane with a bit of a glare, adding "assuming you have time to learn how to use those abilities."

White Crane smiled back but knew Yuraa was already gone and time was short to respond.

"We need to go now," said White Crane. "Kenny and I will fly down to slow your mother and distract your father. Tyson, you and Casey need to get to the stick as quickly as possible. You cannot help us until you get that stick. Are you clear about that?"

"Yes," said Tyson. "We understand. Get the stick first, then we can help you. Got it."

"You must promise me that you won't hurt my dad before we get the stick," begged Tyson.

"We will not hurt your father," said White Crane.

"Casey, will you help Tyson get the polar bear stick?" asked White Crane.

"Yes sir," said Casey angrily. "I will help him."

Casey was still mad about the stick not being hers, but this was Tyson's father and he needed her help. Still, it was tempting. *To be a Flamethrower.*

"Kenny, we must leave now!" urged White Crane.

"Wait! Any tips on how to fly?" asked Kenny sarcastically.

"Close your eyes at first. Feel the owl in the stick." said White Crane. "Let it lead you up on the air. Do short hops at first and go higher as you get confidence."

And with that, White Crane ran towards the edge of the ridge and jumped. The others followed him to the edge and watched. They looked over the steep drop off to see White Crane flying straight down into the mine, like a falcon. His jacket and hair blew hard in the wind as he continued down.

"Better head out, Kenny," said Casey.

"Easy for you to say," said Kenny, his nervousness visible to Casey.

Casey went to her snowmobile slowly. She was still dazed from the fireball earlier. She mounted her snowmobile and took off down the ramp into the mine.

Kenny turned to Tyson. "Casey's left. You better get going too."

Tyson was still trying to process all that had happened in the last two days. Visiting the mine, meeting White Crane, Casey, and Kenny. Finding his father only to realize that he wanted to hurt Tyson. Then seeing fireballs thrown at him, his mother leaving him, and now a man flying to save his dad. What was he doing here? Was this a dream? Was his dad...?

"TYSON!" yelled Kenny. "Get going! Casey and your mom need you! Now!"

Kenny had shaken Tyson out of his confusion. *Yes. Mom needs me.*

"On it!" said Tyson as he jumped onto his snowmobile and took off.

Flamethrowers II

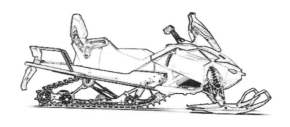

16

Flying

Kenny was nervous and scared about trying to fly. Sure he had the owl stick, but how do you go from standing on the ground to being in the air?

It looked easy when White Crane and even Briggs did it. *Now what did White Crane say? Start with small jumps, right? Then jump longer, and longer.*

Kenny started to run towards the edge of the mine, but as he got closer he realized it was no small jump to the next level. *Maybe I should run on the ramp and start that way.*

Kenny ran down the path and started jumping. He could feel something, but it didn't really take him very far. *Just keep doing it*, thought Kenny. *Just keep jumping.*

Kenny kept running and jumping with little to show for his efforts. He stopped and thought back about how White Crane left the edge of the ridge. White Crane had simply jumped, but that's what Kenny was doing. What else was he missing? *Hadn't White Crane put his arms out? Was that it? Act like you have wings?*

Kenny started to run and jump and this time put his arms wide open as if to grab the air and bammm! Kenny face planted right into the snow and could feel the pain from his face. Ouch… that didn't work.

Struggling to his feet, Kenny again stood silent, wondering what else he could be missing. He closed his eyes and tried to feel the power within the stick. He knew it had power, but he needed a way to transfer it into himself.

White Crane neared Yuraa, who was riding her snowmobile quickly down the mine. White Crane knew he had to stop her before she reached her husband. White Crane saw Blade throwing fireballs at him, trying to slow him down.

He flew right in front of Yuraa, causing her to

slow down in reaction. To White Crane's surprise, she did not stop. He passed in front of her again and again. Each time, she merely slowed down. White Crane was shocked that she was so focused on her husband that the sight of a flying man did not deter her.

Yuraa knew White Crane meant well but she needed to see her husband. It had been years since she had seen him. Did she dare believe that he was alive? Was Tyson right, or was he wishing, hoping to find his dad who had left him?

White Crane could feel his efforts were not going to be successful, so he turned his attention to Blade. Blade had stopped shooting and was standing on the lowest level in the mine. White Crane could now feel the presence of Blade. White Crane could feel the evil below and it slowed him for a moment. He was alone and facing a strong man with the evil polar bear lacrosse stick.

Kenny now felt something. A charge, a strength inside him, began to build. He opened his eyes and began running again. He took a small leap and went a little farther than before. *Okay*, he thought, *I can do this.* Kenny stepped again, again, and again, each time jumping farther. Next step and whammm! Again, face down in the snow. Ouch.

Kenny slowly got up again, his face bleeding from the hard falls. *Ugh, this is not fun.*

Kenny knew he had to focus. He had tapped into some energy but it wasn't clear to him why he fell this time. Kenny got up and walked over to the edge. He wondered how everyone else was doing. *I bet they're doing better than me* he laughed.

He looked down and saw Casey and Tyson riding down deeper in the mine. Yuraa was much further ahead. But where was White Crane?

As Kenny looked around he saw Blade down at the bottom of the mine, and White Crane was flying towards him. *Whoa, I gotta go. He's alone and he's counting on me.*

Kenny closed his eyes and asked for help. "Rakuu, please help me," he said out loud. Kenny had seen Rakuu when Briggs had knocked him out during the battle over the evil owl stick. Rakuu had told him that he would help him on his quest. And Kenny needed help now. White Crane was alone against a powerful evil Flamethrower.

Kenny knelt down on one knee to focus his energy. He got up running, fully committed to leaping as far as he could. As he left the ground he felt something different, a force pushing him, lifting him up. He was flying!

Well he wasn't really flying, but he was jumping really far. Kenny could feel the strength of the stick pushing his body forward. He felt stronger, taking longer jumps and absorbing the impact and lifting off again. He was moving down the mine and going to help White Crane.

Yuraa could now see her husband below. He was simply standing there now. Not crazy like the others described him. Not running around. Not yelling. She was feeling happy to finally see him. She also saw White Crane was close and she needed to go faster. She leaned forward and cranked on the gas. *I can't let him hurt Blade before I get there. He will be so happy to see me*, she thought. *We can be a family again. This will all be over soon.*

White Crane knew he had to reach Blade before the others. White Crane slowed down as he reached the bottom of the mine and held his arms out to keep himself just off the ground.

When Blade did not try to attack him, White Crane landed. The two stood there facing one another.

The ground had only a covering of snow, an inch at the most. The snow was blowing and swirling around, like a dusty old west street.

In his haste to stop Yuraa, White Crane suddenly realized he had no fireballs with him. He had left the backpack on the snowmobiles. He stood there nervous about what could happen if Blade attacked. But Blade did not attack. In fact, he did not even move. He seemed to be sizing up White Crane. Blade looked down at the polar bear stick in his hands. White Crane watched him as he seemed to be listening, learning from the stick.

White Crane felt a strong presence, a feeling, a dark evil coming from Tyson's father. This was the enemy he was going to have to face, and knew it was not the last time he would need to confront this evil. *Be patient,* he told himself. *Calm your mind. Let the evil come. Do not force the confrontation. Be ready. Be ready.*

Up above, Casey and Tyson continued down into the mine. Both were racing as fast as they could to reach Tyson's parents.

Casey looked down and saw that White Crane had reached the lowest level. She saw Blade and White Crane just standing there, facing each other. Casey pointed down towards them. Tyson looked down and saw his dad being calm, not acting crazy or yelling. *Maybe he's okay now* thought Tyson. *Maybe the stick's powers have worn off.*

Casey watched as the two started walking towards each another. Are they speaking to each other? What could he be saying to him? Casey remembered how Briggs could not be reasoned with. He was blind with rage and trying to destroy things. Nobody could talk to Briggs; he would not stay still or listen to anyone. How had White Crane calmed Tyson's dad?

Whamm!

Kenny slammed into the ground near Casey and Tyson.

"I thought you were supposed to be flying?" asked Casey.

Kenny was out of breath as he landed near them. "Yeah! Well I'm started to get the hang of this."

Tyson noticed the blood flowing from Kenny's nose and cheeks. "Yeah." He paused. "You look great!"

Casey turned to Tyson as they both snickered at one another. Casey was smiling; she knew Kenny was not the most athletic kid in the world, either. Why White Crane thought he could just learn to fly was beyond her understanding.

"You'd better go help him, Peter," said Casey.

Tyson and Kenny looked strangely at her.

"Peter Pan... You can fly, You can fly..."

They continued to stare at her.

Casey's knowledge of Disney movies was lost on them. She rolled her eyes.

Kenny sighed. He refocused, began running, then jumped high and over the edge, landing a full level below.

Casey turned around to find that Tyson had taken off, leaving her behind.

17

Showdown

Blade and White Crane stood in the mine like two old west gunslingers. A gray and white snow mix swirled around them. White Crane took a step to his left, not forward to provoke Blade, but wanting to get his attention.

Very slowly, Blade looked up from the stick he had been listening to.

"I know why you are here, old man," said Blade. "But you can't stop me."

"I am not alone," said White Crane.

They stepped to the left and then right, countering each other, but there was no aggression from either side.

"Your son, your wife, they are here with me," said White Crane.

"They are no concern of mine now," said Blade. "I have a destiny. I have a purpose I must fulfill."

"No," said White Crane. "You have a family. A family that misses you."

"The Flamethrowers are my family now."

"The Flamethrowers were the guardians of the game. You are not a Flamethrower. The evil inside the stick will destroy you," said White Crane.

"You can't stop what's coming," said Blade.

"Maybe not, but that time is not now," said White Crane. "My job is not to prevent the future, but protect it."

"Protect it?" said Blade. "Ha! You cannot protect yourself."

With that, Blade took off running at White Crane. White Crane waited. *Patience* he told himself. At the last moment, White Crane pushed off the ground and held a position out Blade's reach.

Blade swung his long lacrosse stick at White Crane, but it was no use, he could not reach him.

White Crane moved away and landed on the ground again. Blade knew he was powerful and could hurt White Crane easily, but his power was worth nothing if he could not reach him.

"A showdown is coming, old man," said Blade. "You know the stories. You know they are true."

"I know our stories. I don't know what stories you have been told," said White Crane.

"There is only one story. The Creator is returning the Flamethrowers to the earth," said Blade. "They will decide who shall rule next. The Creator is giving us both a chance to prove which side is stronger."

"The Creator gives us choice," said White Crane. "Choice and hope. Which choice will you make?"

Blade answered, "People always want choice, but they always choose poorly. We will show the world that our way is the best way. No choice. No will. Only power over the land."

"Your choice is clear," said White Crane. "Lay down your stick, join your son. You will become a powerful leader for us."

"You cannot offer the power you do not have, old man," said Blade. "You are weak; you have nothing to offer me."

"Look up!" said White Crane, pointing to levels above. Your wife and son will soon be here to help you. Return to them. Just lay down the stick."

"They want nothing to do with me," said Blade. "I left them years ago."

White Crane was buying time until Kenny and the others could join him. He knew Kenny would have the fire rocks, and using them the team could hold off Blade, at least for a little while.

White Crane continued with small movements to his left, making Blade follow and focus on him. *Come on Kenny*, thought White Crane, *where are you?*

"Quit stalling and attack me. You want to destroy me, right? Come get me," taunted Blade.

"I don't want to destroy," said White Crane. "Only help."

"You are weak old man, you cannot help me," said Blade.

"I am stronger than you think," said White Crane.

That challenge seemed to get Blade going. He picked up a fire rock from the ground using his long pole. As it caught fire White Crane held his ground. He waited for the shot. Blade could feel the power of the fire in his stick and took a large step forward with his left leg, and shot the fireball directly at White Crane.

The fireball roared loudly out of the stick, sounding like the loud roar of a blaze. It headed directly at the old man. White Crane held out his stick with both hands. As the fireball reached him, he swung the stick at the fireball, deflecting it into the dirt and snow.

Blade was furious now. *Lucky hit* he thought. Again he scooped another fire rock and walked to his right, waiting for it to catch fire. As the rock lit up he shot again, this time at the old man's head. Again, White Crane deflected the shot.

Blade was not done. He scooped another rock, throwing it at White Cloud's feet, hoping to make the deflection more difficult. But White Crane stepped towards the fireball and deflected again before it could hit the ground.

Frustrated by his inability to hit White Crane, Blade tried to distract him. Make him angry. He needed White Crane to attack him, and then he would have an advantage.

"Nice moves, old man," said Blade. 'You have some skill."

White Crane did not respond. *Where are you, Kenny?*

"But you are only delaying the inevitable," said Blade. "You are going to die today. You know you must to save your friends."

White Crane could feel him trying to tempt him, wanting him to attack. He remembered his father teaching him to fish and hunt. Don't chase, let the fish come to you. Set the hook when you're ready, don't force. Of course, like most young sons he lost patience, lost his focus, and lost his catch.

But the memory that haunted him, the one that drove the lesson home, was the time his father was teaching him to hunt a deer. He had shot the deer but it was not a clean shot, and the deer had staggered away.

His father taught him to follow the tracks, to follow the blood, which went on for what seemed like a few miles. Finally they reached the deer, which was now down. But they were not alone. A wolf had reached the deer and was making it his dinner. His young mind was angered by the thought that the wolf felt entitled to his deer. He ran at the wolf. His father yelled, "No! Do not chase him."

It was too late; he took off running at full speed, intending to scare off the wolf. However, he did not scare the wolf; instead, he realized he was the one in trouble.

"Wolves never hunt alone," yelled his father. "Get back here now. Let them have their meal."

He began to back up towards his father. He remembered that you never turn your back on a predator; never show them your backside. He slowly stepped back and lifted his rifle towards the wolf to show that he was a threat. He could hear the other wolves nearby, and his father watched as his son slowly made his way back up the hill.

"Hurry up son," said his father. "We need to leave."

White Crane turned around and realized he was now surrounded. Seeing his son cornered by the wolves, the father now had only one choice to save his son. Raising his rifle, the father shot the first wolf. The wolves cried out but they had the high ground and the numbers. The father shot again, and then again. Three wolves down.

White Crane, who saw that his father had shot three of the wolves, now felt empowered to do the same. He shot one wolf, then another, until the rest ran away.

White Crane remembered feeling relief that he was safe and that he and his father could now get the deer. His father did not feel the same way.

"Your anger got the best of you," said the father. "These wolves did not have to die today. It is your fault they are dead."

"They tried to attack us!"

"They meant you no harm, at first; they only wanted to eat the deer."

"The deer I hunted," he answered angrily.

"No, the deer was theirs at that point," said the father. "You merely helped the Creator provide for them."

White Crane started to understand. He looked around and saw five dead wolves. He and his father did not come out here to do that. His father only killed them to save him, after he had run off. His anger had killed five innocence creatures of the Creator. There was no purpose in that.

His father told him that they would leave the deer for the other wolves. Then he walked him over to the five dead wolves and made him cut the tails off each wolf. He told his son to keep the tails as a reminder of the price of his anger and how others had to suffer from his mistake. White Crane kept those tails and still had them in his desk, bottom drawer, left side.

White Crane looked up and saw Blade trying to taunt him into action. *Patience* he thought, *others are coming, we shall prevail with patience.*

18

Help Arrives

Tyson could hear the sound of the explosions coming from below. He knew that White Crane must be attacking his dad, though White Crane promised he would not hurt him.

Tyson did not stop to look; he just had to get there as fast as he could. Tyson stood up on his sled, trying to take the impacts from the bumps and trenches in the snow. *Faster,* he thought, *faster.* As he looked up, he still could not see his mother. She must be there by now. She must have reached him.

Blade watched as White Crane stood before him, not responding in any way to his threats and insults. He needed White Crane to become angry and fight him on the ground. That would be his advantage, to keep White Crane on the ground.

Slowly Blade started to walk towards him, making very slow moves; if his threats were not going to work, he needed to get closer to grab him. White Crane looked like he was in a trance as he moved slowly forward. Soft step after soft step, the snow and gravel moved and made light sounds.

Almost there, he thought, *almost...* with a long leap and swing of the stick, Blade reached to hit him. Just as his long pole was ready to make contact with White Crane's head, White Crane countered with a quick move of his own stick, deflecting the dark stick away. Crack! You could hear the sticks colliding. White Crane quickly moved his feet back, but Blade was powerful, and reached and grabbed White Crane's jacket.

Quickly White Crane realized that he needed to break Blade's grip on him. White Crane bent down like he was going to jump up. Blade braced himself.

If I try to fly away, I'll have a passenger, he thought. Instead, White Crane kicked his feet in the air sideways, doing a cartwheel that surprised Blade so much that he lost his hold on White Crane and fell. Quickly White Crane landed back on his feet then used his lacrosse stick to poke Blade in the throat. This knocked Blade back a couple of steps. Once he had hit Blade, White Crane quickly retreated into the air.

Blade stumbled back. He knew he had gotten to White Crane, and more importantly White Crane knew it too. Blade watched as White Crane hung in the air, out of reach. Suddenly, Blade heard a snowmobile approach.

Yuraa had finally reached them. She saw a man waving a long stick and White Crane hanging in mid-air. Her focus was not on White Crane flying but the man everyone had told her was her husband. She stopped the snowmobile and sat on it in disbelief. *Was this really him?* She didn't recognize him at first. Something was different.

She was conflicted inside. Was this the man who ran away from his family, left them alone for all these years? Her heart felt anger towards that man.

But was this also the man she mourned for so many years? Was this a chance to be reunited? Her mind and heart wanted answers. Had he been living here all this time alone, not that far from them? Why?

"Is it you?" she weakly asked. "It is really you?"

Blade did not move or answer her. The longer she stood there, the more she wanted to know.

"Why?" she asked. "Why have you been gone so long from us? Why did you leave? Why are you here?"

She had been so focused on getting here that she realized she had no idea what she going to do now that she was in front of him. Her mind was lost in a fog. Her heart felt some hope and yet feared the pain of her husband. What was she going to do now? She stood looking at him, confusion causing her to be still.

Blade had also remained still, but suddenly began running at her. She did not move, but her heart began to pound. *Is he coming to hug me? Reunite with me?*

With alarm, White Crane realized that Yuraa was in danger. He was on the other side of Blade and could not reach her in time. He yelled out to her, "Move! Get out of his way!"

It was too late. She did not understand what was going on, and she did not move away. Blade ran straight at her. He bent down as he reached her snowmobile, and using his new strength, lifted the machine. Yuraa and the machine were flung into the side of the mine. She hit the ground hard. White Crane saw that she was not conscious.

Kenny had fallen over and over in his attempts at a take-off, and as he stood up again he saw the snowmobile tossed into the air. *Whoa,* he thought, *who was that?* Kenny saw the person fly through the air and hit the hillside. He could tell it was not White Crane. But who was it? *I need to get there, I can't give up.* With that, Kenny began running again and taking long leaps.

Tyson had come around the corner in time to see his father run into the snowmobile, sending his mom to the ground. He yelled at his father, "NO!"

Quickly he drove to his mother's side and got off to help her. She had a gash on her head where it hit the snowmobile, and it was bleeding down her face. Tyson grabbed a bandana from his jacket and tied it around her head to stop the bleeding. Casey arrived and rushed over to help Tyson.

"Is she okay?" asked Casey.

"Don't know. She's out."

Tyson turned his attention to his dad. Blade had watched as Tyson and Casey had arrived, and kept his eyes fixed on Tyson. Blade's face underwent a change, making Casey uneasy. The expression went from rage to a more controlled calm. His eyes were still on Tyson.

White Crane was looking around for the source of the fireballs Blade had thrown earlier. He knew he needed to stop Blade from hurting the kids now.

He quickly found the rocks on the ground and flew down to scoop one up. He flew back towards Blade, who was walking towards Tyson and Casey. White Crane threw the fireball right at Blade's feet, causing him to stop and look back.

Tyson was not happy about White Crane shooting at his dad. He yelled up, "You promised not to hurt him."

"He is dangerous, you saw what he did to your mother," answered White Crane. "Casey, you need to keep back." He then turned to grab another fire rock.

Tyson realized that he was very upset with his

father too. "Why did you hurt her?" he demanded. "She came here to help you! I came back to help you!"

Blade did not respond. Tyson kept yelling at his father and began to take steps towards him. Casey realized she had to stop him. She moved in front of Tyson and put her hands on his chest to stop him.

"Stop it!" yelled Casey. "You have to stay away from him!"

"He hurt my mother!" said Tyson. "He hurt me! What do you want from us, father?"

White Crane flew down between Casey and Blade. "Tyson, we need to stay away from him. He is very powerful right now."

"No," said Tyson. "He owes me some answers. Why did you hurt mom?"

"This is not the time," said Casey. "We don't have the good polar bear lacrosse stick. Without it we cannot defeat him."

"Casey is right," said White Crane, trying to plead with Tyson to stop confronting his father.

Casey and White Crane continued to block Tyson from moving towards his dad, and Tyson was growing very frustrated.

Tyson yelled out again, "Dad, talk to me! Tell me

what is going on. I don't know who to believe."

Blade, who had been quietly watching his son struggle against his companions, began to move forward. Reaching his left hand out, he began to talk to his son.

19

Join Me

"Son," began Blade in a very calm voice. "I am sorry. Sorry for everything. I did not intend to hurt you or your mother."

Tyson was surprised by Blade's calm voice. Just a moment ago he was this crazed person, and now he was talking to his dad in a calm voice.

"I am better now," said his dad. "I didn't understand what was happening to me. I was scared."

"Don't listen to him," said Casey. "Remember he

still has the evil stick."

Just then Kenny landed on the level above the group. Kenny saw that Yuraa was the one hurt on the ground. Casey looked okay, and so did Tyson and White Crane. Kenny could hear that Blade was talking to Tyson, though he couldn't make out words.

Kenny moved down to the lower level to join Casey, Tyson, and White Crane. Across the base of the mine stood Blade.

"Son, I have learned I have a destiny to fulfill," said Blade. "I have a purpose that will help bring change to the world. I cannot do it alone. I need you. Join me."

Kenny and Casey were confused. What was Blade talking about? White Crane turned to them. "You cannot believe what he is saying. His mind is not his own now. He is trying to trick you."

Tyson was confused, but he liked the idea of joining his dad. Joining to change the world. They could do it together.

Tyson began to move towards his dad, but before getting in a full step, Casey and Kenny got in his way.

"You are not going over there!" insisted Casey.

"Why not?" demanded Tyson. "I've known you guys, what, one day? And you think I should listen to you and not my father?"

This was exactly what White Crane had feared; a son being loyal to his father even when the father was obviously not himself. "Tyson," said White Crane calmly, "remember what happened yesterday. Remember how he was trying to hurt you, hurt others. He cannot be trusted, even now when he has calmed down."

"Well, maybe the evil wore off?" Tyson tried to justify. "Maybe he is back to normal?"

Blade seized on the moment. "Yes son, yes. I am better now and we can be together, as father and son, changing the world."

Tyson moved again and Kenny and Casey struggled to hold him back. White Crane joined them but knew this would not work for long.

"Kenny," said White Crane. "You need to get Tyson out of here. Take him. Now!"

Casey and White Crane let go of Tyson and Kenny grabbed him with both hands and jumped up an entire level before Blade could react.

"Kenny!" yelled Tyson. "Take me back! I want to be with my father!"

Blade looked up to see his son above him. He was starting to feel his anger growing inside. He wanted his son to join him, to become a part of his quest.

"Bring him back!" Blade yelled up to Kenny. "You have no right to do this, to keep my son from me."

"We are protecting your son," said White Crane.

"From who?" asked Blade.

"From you," answered White Crane.

Blade realized that the two standing in front of him could keep him from getting his son back. He suddenly charged at Casey.

Casey saw him coming and ran behind her snowmobile. That failed to stop Blade, who flipped the snowmobile as easily as before, sending it flying into the side of the mine.

Casey quickly ran towards White Crane. She reached out and grabbed onto him as he lifted off the ground. They landed on the opposite side of the mine from Kenny and Tyson.

Tyson and Kenny were arguing, but Kenny could not control the larger and stronger Tyson. Tyson began to run down the hill, back to his dad.

"Tyson, remember you need to get the polar bear stick. You need to get it now," yelled Kenny.

Tyson began to argue but realized, yeah, that's not a bad idea. If he got the polar bear stick, he and his dad would have the matching sticks. *Why not* he thought?

"Kenny," said Tyson. "You're right; I need to get the stick. Fly me over to the entrance and let me go dig out the stick."

Kenny was excited about Tyson changing his mind. He knew that he alone could not stop Tyson from going back to his dad. Kenny looked over to White Crane and called out, "I'm taking Tyson over to get the stick. I'm leaving the backpack of rocks here. Can you distract Blade?"

With that, Kenny took off his backpack of rocks and left it on the ground. He walked over to Tyson and grabbed him. White Crane flew with Casey ove to the backpack. Casey bent down and opened the pack, pouring its contents of rocks out onto the ground. Quickly White Crane scooped up the first one and shot it at Blade.

Blade saw it coming and deflected the fireball away. He was learning how to control his stick. Blade could feel the power of the polar bear stick and the control that came from using it.

Blade looked over at his son, who had reached the

entrance where the stick was located. He turned to face his son, but another fireball came at him from above. Blade ducked and the fireball flew over him. He needed to deal with White Crane before he could help his son.

The diversion was working and Kenny and Tyson ran inside the entrance to retrieve the lacrosse stick. White Crane, now armed with a pack full of rocks, was using them to distract Blade.

Blade looked for rocks near him. He scooped one up and returned fire up the hill. His accuracy still needed improvement, so White Crane and Casey did not worry much about being hit. They watched the first one fly way over their heads.

White Crane continued the barrage of fireballs towards Blade to keep him busy. The fireballs were exploding to the left and right of Blade as he deflected them over and over again.

Blade was starting to feel confident as the fireballs rained down on him. He was deflecting them easily and started to move towards White Crane, up the hill.

The plan was working but White Crane and Casey had hoped to just keep Blade busy while Kenny and

Tyson reached the entrance, not to lure Blade up the hill.

At first, Kenny struggled with Tyson's extra weight, which made flight much harder than it already was. Fortunately, it wasn't far to the entrance behind Blade, and Kenny landed, a bit hard. They tumbled, slamming into the side of the mine.

"Ouch!" Tyson said as he got up. "Nice landing."

"Sorry," said Kenny. "Still getting used to that whole flying thing."

Tyson got up and immediately went into the cave. Sunset was coming fast, and it was getting harder to see. Tyson grabbed the lanterns they'd found earlier, and got them going. Kenny saw the black coffin-like box again. *It's huge*, he thought, looking again at the detail of the polar bear carvings.

Tyson wanted the stick and walked to the table, grabbing a pick ax along the way. He climbed up onto the table and began swinging the pick over his head, again and again. The white container in the ceiling of the cave was being revealed.

As Kenny grabbed a shovel to help Tyson, he heard a voice. Kenny paused to listen but got hit by a rock dislodged by Tyson's digging above him. He moved towards the entrance of the cave and heard the voice again, but it was faint. He stepped farther out to hear better.

He heard Casey yelling. "Help!"

Casey saw Kenny as he came out of the cave and yelled again. "Kenny! He's coming up after us!"

Kenny saw Blade climbing the slope, getting closer to White Crane and Casey. White Crane was focused on throwing the fireballs at Blade, but Blade didn't seem concerned about them. He kept coming without slowing at all.

Kenny flew towards Casey. This time it was much more than a leap. He was actually flying. Without stopping, landing, or losing speed he reached out and grabbed Casey.

Casey held on as Kenny turned away and flew to the other side of the mine. Kenny looked back at White Crane, who had flown into the air just as Blade had missed them

"That was close," said Kenny while catching his breath.

"How's Tyson doing?" asked Casey. "Does he have the stick yet?"

"No," said Kenny. "He was still digging when I heard you."

Casey said, "Take me down there and I can help him."

Casey still really wanted the stick. She thought that if she could get near it, that maybe she might have a chance to get it. Tyson was obviously confused, and the stick was making it worse. So, she told herself that it would be better for everyone involved if she got the stick instead of Tyson.

White Crane yelled out, "Get down and help Tyson get that stick!"

Kenny grabbed Casey and flew right into the entrance of the cave. As Kenny let go of Casey he asked her, "How is White Crane doing?"

Casey answered, "He was shooting a lot of fireballs and getting tired. That's why I yelled for you to help."

"I'd better go back and help him," said Kenny. "You okay helping Tyson?"

Perfect! Casey thought. *Without Kenny, it will be easier to get the stick.* "Sure, go help him."

Kenny looked up and saw that Tyson was making good progress; the white container was nearly dug out. He then turned and ran out to help White Crane.

Casey ran over to Tyson and grabbed a shovel.

She jumped onto the table, and looked at Tyson. She didn't say a word, but simply started to dig away at the dirt around the white coffin-like box.

As Kenny walked out into the light, he did not see White Crane or Blade. It was quiet. Very quiet. Too quiet. Kenny wondered if White Crane might be hurt or hiding from Blade.

Where are they?

20

Baby Blue

Kenny walked out into the open area, and carefully looked around to see where Blade and White Crane had gone. He started to feel a sense of panic. Only seconds had passed, but now Kenny could hear his heartbeat in his ears. The loud pounding sound was causing panic to set in. *Had something happened to White Crane?*

Kenny could not bear the thought of it. He bent down and flew into the air to look for him. As

Kenny went up he noticed right away White Crane's lacrosse stick lying in the open on the hillside. Kenny looked around to find him, but no luck. Kenny knew White Crane would need his stick so he quickly flew down to grab it. As Kenny approached the stick he noticed a small cave. He could see a figure inside.

"Kenny," called out the voice.

He knew immediately it was White Crane.

"Hand me my stick."

Kenny bent down and picked up the lacrosse stick and handed it towards the figure in the dark. White Crane reached out and wrapped his fingers around it, causing the stick to glow and light the small cave where he was hiding.

"Got a little too close," grimmaced White Crane.

White Crane's face looked pale; he had a small cut on his forehead and looked weak and shaky.

"You okay?" asked Kenny. "Yeah, I'm an old man. I don't move so quick anymore. Feel like an old bear struggling to find his way."

"Where'd he go?" asked Kenny.

"Not sure, he caught me by surprise," said White Crane. "I stumbled into here to hide and recover."

Kenny looked around and could not see Blade, but given White Crane's lack of mobility he decided to stay there and not put either one of them out in the open. Hopefully Tyson will get the stick soon and could help them.

Back in the cave, Casey and Tyson had dug out most of the white container. *It must be ready to fall,* thought Tyson.

On the next swipe of the ax, the large white container slipped a couple of inches. They could hear the rock giving way. But then the container stopped and hung in placed.

"Just a couple more hits," said Tyson.

Casey still wanted the stick. *How am I going to convince him to give to me?*

Tyson was silent. *I almost have the stick, Dad. I will be ready to join you.*

They kept swinging away, but the earth was not letting go of the container. The box was hanging in the air with almost no part left lodged in the rock above. *What's holding it in?* wondered Tyson.

Finally, Tyson lost his patience and shoved his weight against the side of the white box. He grabbed ahold and used his weight, swaying side to side to loosen the box. As he swung back and forth in small motions, the box slipped and began to fall.

Casey, caught off guard, tried to jump off the table to get out of the way. Her ankle gave out and she fell to the ground, landing hard on her back. Pain ran down her legs, and she looked up just as one end of the container started to come down right at her. She had less than a second to decide what to do, and she was dazed from her fall.

WHAM! The first end of the box hit the ground flat, lifting dirt and debris into the air. Seconds later, the second half of the box slammed down.

Casey felt stunned and struggled to breathe. She'd managed to choose the right direction to roll away from the box, but she felt dazed and...tired. Very tired.

Tyson waved his arms to disperse the dust in the air, and moved quickly to find the top end of the container. White Crane had given him instructions about how to open the lid. He needed to find the paw with seven claws. It was still tough to see, so he rubbed his hands over the white surface, counting each claw. As he reached the far end of the container, he counted out seven claws.

"That's it!" he exclaimed.

Tyson moved his hand to the center claw and

pressed it upward.

CLICK.

He heard the sound and a small opening became visible on his side of the box.

Casey could hear Tyson moving around and talking to himself, but she was dazed and struggling to get to her feet. When she heard the click she knew he had found a way to open it.

"NO!" she cried out.

It was too late. Tyson had reached his hand into the box and was searching for the stick. He knelt down to deepen his reach, and suddenly felt his fingers brush the stick. He grabbed onto it tightly, as White Crane had told him.

"Ahhhhhhhhhhhh!" yelled Tyson.

He felt the hot burning of the stick in his hand and arm. After several seconds, he passed out.

Casey, gaining her strength, crawled over to Tyson. He was knocked out and lying on the ground, his hand still inside the slot of the container.

She looked down, her mind filling with anger that she hadn't had a chance to grab the stick before Tyson. She sat upon the box and saw that the lid had slid partially open.

Casey peered inside and saw a beautiful baby blue

stick. She pushed the stone lid slowly off one end. It made the grinding noise of stone on stone. The lid was too long to be pushed off on one side alone, so she walked down to the other side and slowly slid the remainder off.

The sound of the lid hitting the ground was nothing compared to the loud crash moments ago. More dust flew into the air.

The sound woke Tyson.

"What happened?" asked Tyson.

Tyson was clearly confused, just like Kenny was when he found the owl stick. But she knew the stick was bonded to him and would not work for her.

Still, she admired the stick, and the smooth blue bones of polar bear that made up the shaft.

The head of the stick was covered in beautiful white fur, with polar bear teeth surrounding the outside of the pocket.

Tyson stood up, looking over Casey's shoulder. "Wow, that is amazing," he said, in awe.

They both stared at it for a moment, and Casey reached first to grab the stick. It was cold to the touch. Casey did not lift the stick: she was checking to see if it might glow for her. It did not. She dropped her head in disappointment.

Tyson reached below her hand and touched the stick. Immediately the stick began to shine with a baby blue glow that lit up the entire cave. It was so bright that Casey covered her eyes at first. They'd been working in the dimly lit cave with just a small lantern.

Tyson picked up the lacrosse stick. It was heavy, and he could feel that it belonged to him. It was comfortable, balanced, and seemed to follow his movements.

Tyson walked toward the exit of the cave. He needed to get outside. Casey watched as Tyson left the cave, alone.

Blade moved down to the lower level again after not seeing where White Crane had gone. He wanted to get inside the cave and help his son. Tyson emerged from the cave with the long lacrosse stick lighting the way.

"Son!" yelled Blade. "You found it!"

Tyson looked up and saw his dad on the other side of the level. Tyson was still a bit confused after being knocked out. But yes, it was his dad, and Tyson felt some pride that his dad seemed proud of him. Still, he felt that something was off.

"Dad, what's going on?"

"Come here, join me."

Tyson started walking towards his father. Suddenly a fireball came flying in from above, just in front of Tyson, knocking him back. Blade and Tyson saw Kenny and White Crane a few levels above them.

"Stay back, Tyson," warned Kenny.

"Tyson, you are with us now," said White Crane.

Tyson was confused. His dad was right here. Why should they care if he wants to be with his dad?

White Crane looked at Kenny and said, "We need to get closer, but stay a level above them. Keep the higher ground. We cannot challenge them on the same level. They are both too powerful for us."

Kenny nodded and took off, flying down to the level above Tyson. White Crane gently landed next to Kenny.

"Tyson," called out White Crane. "Close your eyes and let the stick speak to you."

Tyson, again confused, replied, "The stick is mine old man. I can feel it belongs to me."

"I know," said White Crane. "Let it speak to you."

"Tyson," said Blade. "Come join me now. We can listen to the stick later. Join me ..."

WHAM!

A fireball hit right in front of Blade. Kenny had thrown the fireball to keep Blade from talking to Tyson. The father stood there looking up at Kenny and White Crane, trying to figure out his options. He could not reach them quickly, and they were not coming down to challenge him.

Tyson sensed the stick was trying to communicate with him. A feeling of calm came over him and he closed his eyes. Tyson's mind drifted and his body felt the power of the stick running through him. The stick was talking to him.

As this calm spread over him, he also began to feel something else. The joy he'd so recently felt at finding the second stick was leaving him. In its place was more of a realization that he was feeling pain. Not his own pain, but pain coming from Blade. The man was his father, but was not the father he knew. His father was a warm, gentle man. The person before him was in pain. He was angry, and dangerous. Tyson opened his eyes and looked down at the stick in his hands.

White Crane watched as Tyson transformed in front of him. Tyson was no longer confused. He knew he had to help the others. His job was to stop this evil and he had the tool to do it.

21

Falling Crane

Casey walked around the white box, rubbing her hand on the cold surface. She looked at the carvings and the images. *How did I get caught up in all this? Why am I here?* she wondered. She was not a Flamethrower, not overly smart, nor clever. She just liked to play hockey and compete. Oh, yeah, and she hated to lose.

Casey did like that she had come along. Meeting White Crane had brought her into a new world.

Maybe a world she didn't belong in, but nonetheless a new world of wonder. She admired White Crane and loved his stories. She was intrigued by his completely different view of the world.

Enough drowning in my sorrows, she thought. *Better get back and help.* With that she turned and walked out of the cave.

Yuraa was coming around, groaning and dazed. She didn't remember how she had gotten there. As she looked up she saw that she was not far from Blade. She realized it was her husband.

"Blade!" she called out.

He turned around and saw her struggling to get up.

"Help me!" she pleaded. "I'm hurt."

Blade started to move towards her, but Tyson yelled out, "Stay away from her!"

Yuraa was surprised to hear her son's voice. She had not seen him yet and he too was there with her.

"Son," said Yuraa. "I need help."

"Stay there, mom. Dad is not himself right now."

Blade turned back to Tyson.

"Careful son," said Blade. "You should not challenge me."

"You are evil," said Tyson. "You are not my father."

Yuraa was trying to make sense of the situation. Blade and Tyson arguing made no sense to her. She tried hard to get onto her feet. She was dizzy and her head hurt.

"Do not do this," said Yuraa to her son. "We are a family again. Please calm yourselves and let's go home."

Tyson knew that this was what his mother wanted, to be a family again. With all they had been through, she just wanted everyone together again.

"I know mother, but see that stick in his hands?" Tyson asked, pointing towards his father. "It is evil and has taken control of him. He is not Dad. He is not himself. We cannot go home until we get it from him."

Yuraa looked at Blade and could not see what Tyson was seeing.

"Son, of course we need to help him. We can take him home and help him."

Tyson was feeling that strong sense of calm, something only a mother can do. *Maybe we could just go home and talk this out.* With that, Tyson relaxed his grip on the stick, and let one end rest on the ground.

He drew in a deep breath and looked at his dad.

"Dad," said Tyson. "Let's go home."

It was a simple gesture to calm the situation.

Kenny watched as Yuraa approached Tyson, and as Tyson lowered his lacrosse stick. *This is not going to end well,* thought Kenny.

Just then Blade started to run towards Tyson. Kenny knew he had to act. He was far away, but if he flew straight at Tyson maybe he could reach him in time.

Kenny bent down to leap, but a force hit him, knocking him onto his back. He felt the wind get knocked out of his body and he gasped for air. *What the...*

Tyson saw Blade running at them, so stepped in front of his mother. Wanting to protect her, he lowered his body down, bending his knees.

As Tyson prepared for impact, he realized that Blade was not just running at him, but that he had his stick pulled back, preparing to take a huge swing at them. Tyson was unsure how he was going to block this attack and protect his mother.

Kenny looked up to realize the force that had

knocked him to the ground was White Crane taking off at tremendous speed, flying at Blade. It was like a blur from his viewpoint on the ground as White Crane went directly between Blade and Tyson.

White Crane arrived just as Blade delivered his blow. The crane lacrosse stick had taken the blow and White Crane crashed uncontrollably to the ground.

As White Crane landed, dust and dirt flew up into the air. The moment became silent as White Crane just lay there. Nobody moved. The group only stared in disbelief.

Casey had just walked out of the cave when she saw White Crane get hit by Blade. She felt a shiver of horror go down her back. She said nothing but simply froze in place. She watched in shock, not knowing what to do. *What just happened?*

Kenny could not believe what he saw. White Crane was down on the ground and not moving.

"NO!" yelled Kenny.

His reaction was much more vocal than Casey's. He began screaming at Blade. "Stay away from him! Come get me! Come get me!"

Tyson was stunned that he hadn't been hit. He slowly opened his eyes only to see White Crane lying on the ground. He didn't see the impact that sent him to the earth, and he was surprised that White Crane had moved in front of him.

Tyson pushed his mother back and shoved her away from Blade and towards the cave entrance. Tyson saw that Casey was in shock, staring at White Crane on the ground.

"He's not moving," gasped Casey desperately. "Why isn't he moving?"

"Why did he attack us?" asked Yuraa.

"It's not Dad," said Tyson. "He is not himself. It's like he's possessed. We've been trying to tell you!"

"How can he be possessed?" asked his mom.

"I don't know," said Tyson. "But something is evil inside him. I can feel it."

"We're bringing him home," said Yuraa. "We're bringing him home."

Yuraa was trying to convince herself that everything was going to be okay. However, she clearly did not understand what was going on.

"We need to help him," said Casey. "We need to get to him, protect him."

Tyson wasn't focused on White Crane. He heard Casey, but his thoughts were focused on protecting his mom.

"He still isn't moving!" cried Casey frantically.

She seemed to be the only one focused on badly injured White Crane. She wished he'd do something, anything, to let her know he was alive. She could not hear Kenny yelling from above, as he tried to distract Blade.

"I'm up here!" Kenny yelled at Blade. "Come get me!"

Kenny moved around, waving his arms. He kept his focus on getting Blade away from everyone else so they could reach White Crane.

Blade picked up a fire rock and held it for a few moments. As it caught fire, he moved towards Tyson as Kenny desperately tried to keep Blade's attention.

Kenny turned around to scoop up a fire rock to shoot at Blade. Just as Kenny had turned around, Blade shot a fireball right at Kenny.

"Kenny!" screamed Casey.

As he turned back to Casey, he saw the fireball heading right for him. The fireball landed at his feet, exploding and sending Kenny flying against the side of the mine, where he collapsed.

22

Sad Eyes

Blade turned towards his son. He took a step, then another, moving across the snow and gravel. Tyson watched as his dad slowly came at him. He didn't want his mother to get hurt again, and he kept pushing her back and away from Blade.

"Stay back, mom," urged Tyson.

Blade continued slowly towards them. "I'm not going to hurt you son. I want you to join me."

"You attacked us!" argued Tyson. "You are not my father."

Tyson looked at his father's eyes. They were empty eyes, with flames dancing in the background.

Tyson didn't see his father inside there. He knew the person talking was not his dad.

"If you don't want to join me, than give me the stick," said Blade.

"No!" said Tyson. He realized the stick might be the only thing he could use to protect himself.

Yuraa began to understand that they were in danger. Her thoughts turned to getting her son to safety now. "Tyson, we need to leave."

"We can't leave him like this," said Tyson. "I'm not leaving my dad here like this."

"Tyson," said Casey, "we can't leave White Crane alone. You need to get your father out of here, away from us."

Yuraa was angry with Casey for asking Tyson to help with White Crane. Her mind was to get her son to safety. Let the others deal with Blade.

"Do not tell my son what to do," growled Yuraa. "We need to leave here, now."

Tyson knew his father was not going to just let him leave, to just walk out of there. "Mom, please just stay here!"

"No!" insisted Yuraa.

"Casey, when you get the chance, check on White

Crane," said Tyson.

Casey nodded.

Tyson raised his lacrosse stick in both hands and squeezed it tight. He said to the stick, "I need whatever power you can give me."

With that he moved quickly towards his dad, swinging his stick. He had not learned how to throw the fireballs yet and was using his stick like a sword.

Blade stepped back to absorb the blow with his own stick. A clashing sound rang out as the sticks smashed into each other. Good versus evil colliding for the first time in centuries.

Blade moved back then attacked Tyson with a swipe of his stick. Tyson blocked his attack but was forced back several feet.

"Good, son," said Blade. "Hit me."

Tyson was not listening. He needed his energy focused on moving his father away, on getting the others to safety.

Tyson lunged and attacked Blade, again and again. He rushed, he hit, he slashed at his father. Each time, the attacks were blocked. Tyson was growing tired from the contact.

Casey looked around and realized that there were fire rocks on the ground. She picked one up and threw it to Tyson.

"Catch," she yelled.

It sailed past Tyson's stick. No lacrosse skills yet. Tyson watched as the rock rolled behind him.

"Scoop it up," said Casey. "It will catch fire and you can shoot it at him."

Tyson backed up a few steps and reached with his long stick to scoop the rock off the ground. "Got it. Now what do I do?"

Casey instructed, "Hold it for a few seconds. You will hear it catch fire, then shoot it at him."

"I don't want to kill him," said Tyson.

"Shoot for his feet, force him back," she yelled to him. "You have to back him up."

Tyson pulled the lacrosse stick up with the pocket behind his head. Blade stood his ground, not moving. Tyson heard the rock catch fire, and pulled the stick hard to shoot the fireball at his dad. Tyson could feel it go sideways and leave the stick early. Whoosh, the fireball flew up into the air and landed on the level above.

Blade watched as the fireball sailed away from his son. He then looked around to find a rock to throw back.

Casey tossed another rock to Tyson, "Try again."

Tyson missed catching the rock again, but quickly scooped it. He saw his father looking around on the ground and sent a warning shot over Blade's head.

Blade knew Tyson's aim was getting better. He scooped another rock and turned back to his son.

Yuraa saw that Blade had a fireball and was going to shoot it at their son. Her instinct was clear and she ran between them to stop her husband.

"NO!" screamed Yuraa.

Her head was pounding from being knocked out earlier and from the panic of her son being attacked. Her plea did not stop Blade from firing. The fireball flew right at her, hitting her in the chest. Hard.

Yuraa collapsed to the ground.

Casey tried to yell but nothing came out. First White Crane, now Yuraa. This was too much. This wasn't supposed to happen.

Tyson caught his mother as she collapsed and he fell to the ground with her. He reached to his mother's face to see her eyes; he wanted to see that she was okay. But her head fell in his arms, and her eyes showed no life.

"NO!" screamed Tyson. "NO! How could you?"

Tyson held his mother tight, embracing her on the ground, refusing to let her go. Maybe if he held her tight enough she would come back.

Kenny bolted upright, taking a great gasp. He had been knocked out by the fireball and woke up struggling to breathe.

Kenny took in the precious air, trying to gain his strength back. He looked down, seeing himself covered in dirt and snow. *What happened?* he thought. He rolled over on his side and tried to lift himself up, but he became dizzy and crashed back to his hands and knees.

He started to remember that he'd been hit by a fireball. *Casey,* he thought. *Where is Casey?*

Kenny saw his owl stick nearby; he crawled over to the stick and pushed himself up again, using the lacrosse stick to steady himself.

He looked down below and saw White Crane still on the ground, not moving. Then he heard Tyson yelling at his father. Kenny realized Tyson was holding his mother in his arms. *This wasn't supposed to happen,* he thought. *We were supposed to help rescue the father.*

Kenny saw Casey hiding near the entrance to the cave. She looked scared. *Casey is never scared,* thought

Kenny. This actually scared him a little.

With his strength returning, Kenny grabbed his backpack then bent down to take flight into the mine. Kenny flew, with good control, landing right in front of Tyson and his mom.

Tears were streaming down Tyson's face. Kenny then looked at the lifeless face of Yuraa.

Kenny gasped, but the sound came out in a whisper, "Nooo."

Tyson looked up at Kenny, "He killed my mom! He killed my mom!"

Casey yelled out, "LOOK OUT!"

Kenny spun around just as Blade threw a fireball right at the group. Kenny's instincts were to fly away but he knew Tyson would get hit, so he turned his lacrosse stick to deflect the shot like he'd seen White Crane do.

WHAM!

Kenny managed to get most of it, but he was not set and the impact threw him to the ground. Kenny quickly recovered and dropped the pack from his back, spilling fire rocks onto the ground.

Kenny scooped one and fired back quickly. It failed to have much of an impact because he'd thrown too soon. He reminded himself to be more patient.

Blade called out, "You don't have the strength to defeat me, little one. Your size is no match for the strength of the polar bear."

Kenny ignored him and threw a couple more fireballs, this time forcing Blade up and away from Tyson and Casey.

"Casey," called Kenny, "when we get him out of here you need to check on White Crane. Get to him, help."

Casey nodded. She was still scared, but she knew Kenny was right. She called back now with confidence growing inside her. "Will do. Be careful."

"The old man is dead too, little girl," taunted Blade.

Kenny was growing angry. He screamed back, "Shut up!" Not very witty or convincing. He was too scared and his head hurt so much from being knocked out earlier.

"What are you going to do, boy?" laughed Blade. "You can't beat me. Back off and let me get my son. We will leave you here to die with the others."

Tyson, grieving as he held his mother in his arms, listened to his father mock Kenny. Tyson's anger grew in his grief, and he felt that he needed to kill Blade.

He gently set his mother down onto the ground and picked up his lacrosse stick. Kenny saw Tyson getting up and walked carefully back to him.

"You need to take the shot," said Kenny. "He is too powerful for me alone."

Tyson walked past Kenny, saying nothing.

"Scoop a fireball and be ready," said Kenny. "I will distract him."

But Tyson didn't react. He was confused.

Kenny's mind was spinning. There wasn't time to help Tyson sort this out. He needed Tyson to be throwing fireballs. To help, Kenny put a fire rock into the stick pouch.

"Once it ignites, throw it at your dad!" said Kenny, trying to engage Tyson.

He gave Tyson another reassuring look, and could only hope that Tyson would do his part. Kenny bent down and pushed hard, and flew directly towards Blade to distract him from Tyson's (hopefully) incoming fireball.

But Kenny miscalculated how fast he was going, and flew too close to Blade.

Blade reached out with the long stick, swinging it

at the boy flying at him. Kenny turned upward as quickly as he could, but he was too low. Blade caught him right on the back as he passed, sending Kenny slamming into the side of the mine.

Tyson knew this was his chance. Kenny had distracted Blade. Now Tyson had his own job to do. This time the shot would not be just a warning. Tyson's anger was too strong after losing his mother. This would be a direct shot at his father. Tyson drew his stick back, far back, and let loose a shot with all he had. The shot went directly at his father.

Tyson watched as the fireball headed straight for his dad. He felt that his anger was justified. He wanted to hurt his father, make him suffer for taking his mother away from him. Tyson was hoping his father would not turn around after hitting Kenny, and that the fireball would hit him with no time to try to deflect it.

But Blade did turn around, and although he could not react fully in time to deflect the shot, he was able to get his stick on the fireball and absorb some of the energy. The hit was strong though, and Blade was thrown back. The fireball had caught him high against his shoulder. He fell to the ground, dropped the stick, and rolled to try to extinguish his burning clothes. Then things went black.

Casey left the entrance of the cave and ran towards White Cane. She grabbed him and turned him onto his side. She gasped in fear as his head rolled back. Then she saw his eyes open.

Flamethrowers II

23

Take It

Casey exhaled and took a deep breath. *He's alive,* she thought. *He's alive!* She was so excited with relief!

She knelt by his side, and moved him onto his back. White Crane just moaned. He was clearly in a lot of pain.

Casey sat there holding his hand for what felt like the longest time. "It's going to be okay," she told him.

White Crane managed to move his lips a bit; not quite a smile, but certainly the intent was there.

"With you here, I'm sure everything is going to be okay." White Crane tried to lift his head and shoulders, but a weakness he had not felt in a long time kept him held down.

Casey could see the strain on his face. "Don't move, no need to get up. Tyson and Kenny are fine." She lied. She knew Kenny was hit again and Tyson's anger seemed to have the best of him. She didn't mention Yuraa, either.

White Crane laid back down.

"Yuraa. She okay?" he struggled to ask.

Casey paused; there was no easy way to say it. So she didn't. White Crane looked into Casey's eyes. He knew. He seemed to read even more into her non-answer, and asked, "Are you okay?"

Casey teared up, but did not respond. She was feeling for the first time in her young life that she didn't know what was going to happen next. Her past told her she was in control of things. Tryouts, making the team, scoring a goal, hanging out with the Conley family. She made things happen.

Now she was facing a situation where she didn't have control, where she had to rely on others, and where she was helpless to defeat the person causing the pain. Her heart felt heavy.

White Crane saw the struggle in Casey's face. The weight of the world seemed to be on her. *Why is she feeling this burden?* he wondered.

He tried to sit up again, and again his strength failed him. Fading back down he asked, "Kenny. How is he doing?"

She paused but answered, "He is hurt, and Tyson is angry at his father for killing his mom."

"Help is coming," said White Crane.

Casey heard what he said, but it made no sense to her. Who would be coming? They had no way to communicate. Cell phones didn't work out here. She assumed that he was just delirious from the injuries.

White Crane lifted his right arm, the one holding the crane lacrosse stick. "Take it."

Now Casey knew he was not in his right mind. He wouldn't just offer his stick. *He thinks he is going to die.*

"No," answered Casey, alarm in her voice. "No. Don't even say that."

"You need to help them, Casey."

"No! We need you. You can't leave us."

Casey's heart was now racing with the rush of adrenaline in her veins. Yes she wanted a Flamethrower stick. But to get White Crane's lacrosse stick required him to die to pass it on.

Casey's heart was too torn apart to lose another person today. "NO! You are not going to die today."

White Crane held the stick up higher, his arm shaking from weakness. "Take it!"

Casey shook her head and refused to reach for it.

"We need you. You guided us here, you will guide us home."

"I am an old man. This is not an old man's quest. Please, you must save Kenny and Tyson."

With all the courage she could find in her heart she said, "We will find a way. Together, we will find a way. Now is not your time to leave us. We won't know where to go next without you. It is you who have to show us the way."

White Crane tried another smile. "Casey, I am not the only one who knows the stories and places to go. There are others who can help you on this odyssey."

"I don't want any others; I want you to show us the way."

She was determined and stubborn. White Crane already knew that and even felt amused, seeing that she was now going to try to push away his death. He rolled back the weight of his body and relaxed. *If I do die, at least the stick will be near her.*

Casey, seeing White Crane relax, knew he was not

going to fight her anymore. Her tears began to fall again, and she yelled out, "Help!"

Blade, who had been knocked out for a moment, woke up realizing his clothes were still smoldering.

Tyson stood there staring in anger at Blade. He was gripping the stick so hard that as he absently turned it in his hands, it made a squeaking sound.

Blade's stick was beside him on the ground, where he'd dropped it when he tried to put out his burning clothes. Tyson noticed that the stick, which had earlier glowed with a dark light, now simply looked black, with bones and fur to match.

Tyson felt he needed to attack again, before his father could regain the stick and his strength. Tyson turned to find a fire rock.

"Osseo!"

What? thought Tyson. *What did Dad just say?*

Tyson felt faint suddenly, as his anger drained away and left a feeling of shock.

"Osseo! I'm sorry. I'm so sorry."

Tyson didn't know what to think. His brother was dead from the polar bear attack years ago. Why was Blade calling Osseo's name?

"It's my fault," yelled Blade desperately. "I had to choose. I had to ..." his voice failed him. Blade was on his hands and knees.

Tyson looked around in confusion. But there were no visible ghosts. But something was haunting his father.

"I'm so sorry Osseo," sobbed Blade.

Tyson's anger was now turning to guilt. He was the one his dad had saved. His father had sacrificed Osseo for him.

Tyson lowered his stick and listened to his father's torment.

Kenny had slammed into the hillside behind Blade. His back hurt from being tagged by Blade's polar bear stick. He slowly made his way onto his feet and heard the blast as Tyson had hit his father, knocking him to the ground. Kenny tried to fly over to Tyson, but a sharp pain in his back caused him instead to drop back to his knees.

Kenny listened for a moment as Blade spoke to Tyson. While he couldn't make out the words, he took advantage of each moment to regain strength.

Tyson stood there, holding his lowered stick. Kenny then looked over at Blade, who was on his hands and knees, crying out and screaming about Osseo. *Who is Osseo?* wondered Kenny.

Kenny then noticed that Blade had dropped this stick. *Yes!* thought Kenny. *We're almost home.*

Kenny yelled out to Tyson, "He's dropped the stick! We need to get it away from him!"

Kenny started running towards Blade. Kenny called out, "Remember not to touch the evil stick with your hands! Use your stick or something else, but do not ..."

Blade turned around to see Kenny running at him. Blade was confused. Who was this? He turned back to Osseo, but his vision had ended. Instead, he saw Tyson. He felt weak, feeling the loss again.

The effects of the evil stick were wearing off, but Blade had no idea what was going on. He looked back and forth at these two kids, and tried to make sense of the moment.

Hearing Kenny telling Tyson to get the dark stick, he assumed that the stick was his only chance to defend himself against Kenny.

As Blade reached for the stick, Kenny and Tyson both yelled out, "NO!"

But it was too late. Blade had reached out and grabbed the stick. He felt a sudden rush of pain, then suddenly no pain. He stood up and raised the stick to the sky. He let out a loud roar that reverberated against the walls of the mine.

Oh no, thought Kenny. And he was right. Blade had healed and was as strong as ever. *The stick must have some healing powers*, thought Kenny.

Tyson scooped up a fire rock and paused to wait for it to ignite. Kenny was right; the stick seemed to change the person who held it.

Tyson knew he had to get the stick from his father. As soon as the fireball started, Tyson threw a direct shot at his dad, right at his head. Blade dropped to one knee and the shot flew right over him, but Kenny was right behind Blade and had to leap away to avoid being hit.

Whammmm! The fireball exploded into the hillside.

"Help!" yelled Casey again.

Kenny looked over and saw Casey kneeling by White Crane's side. They were not too far away and Kenny could see the look of terror in Casey's eyes.

Kenny ran towards Casey, thinking, *Tyson can hold him off for a few minutes*. Kenny reached them and knelt down to look at White Crane.

"He's hurt bad," said Casey.

"What should we do?" asked Kenny.

Tyson's anger had returned. The person in front of him now was not his dad. He knew this. He knew this person had killed his mom.

Blade and Tyson started to circle one another.

What's next? thought Tyson as he tried to plan his next move.

Tyson noticed that Blade didn't seem to be planning to shoot any fireballs. It was going to be a battle of sticks. Tyson felt a huge power inside him and took the first step. Blade reacted and soon both were running at each other at full speed.

Casey looked up and saw the two running towards each other. "We better get out of here, this doesn't look good."

"Can we move him?" wondered Kenny.

Blade and Tyson collided. The force of the two sticks colliding sent shock waves in all directions. It was like a blast the mine had never seen before. Echoes of sound reached out.

Casey and Kenny were knocked down. The force of the blast was intense and everyone was now on their backs, looking at the darkening sky.

You could hear the gravel, snow, and dirt shaking above them. Casey felt horror as she yelled out, "LANDSLIDE!"

24

Collapse

Kenny looked up and saw what Casey was warning them about. Snow and dirt was pouring down the sloped sides from the higher levels, threatening to trap them at the lowest level of the mine. Kenny moved to White Crane and picked him up. He was very heavy for Kenny to lift, but he knew they had to get all of them out.

"OK I'm ready. Casey, jump on my back!" Kenny said. "We have to get out of here."

Casey jumped onto Kenny's back. She saw the crane lacrosse stick slipping from White Crane's hand. She grabbed his hand and helped close it around the stick.

"We are going to need all the flying power we can get," said Casey as she looked into White Crane's eyes. "We need your help."

With that, Kenny pushed off, carrying the weight of White Crane and Casey. At first it seemed he was not even leaving the ground. Then, as if someone was pushing his feet, they moved into the air. *Must be White Crane pushing me*, he thought.

Kenny directed himself upwards to the center of the mine opening, as the walls seemed to be collapsing around them. He watched as the snow and dirt fell into the levels below. Kenny's thoughts turned to Tyson. *How is he going to survive this?*

The earth continued to fall from above. The sound was like distant thunder in a summer storm. The whole place was shaking, collapsing onto itself.

Finally the sound stopped and Kenny looked around for a place to safely land. He noticed a ridge sticking out that looked like it survived the landslide.

"Slowly he moved the three of them to the ridge and ever so gently laid White Crane onto the ground.

Casey rolled off Kenny's back and the three of them were all grateful to be on the ground again.

"What happened?" asked White Crane weakly.

"Blade and Tyson ran at each other, colliding and sending out shock waves, or something, that triggered a landslide," said Casey.

"Two powerful forces," said White Crane.

Kenny looked over the ridge to the areas below. The dust was still settling. He could not see the ground below.

"I can't see anything," said Kenny.

"Do you think…" asked Casey as her voice trailed off. She didn't want to finish her question.

Kenny and Casey sat on the edge of the ridge, waiting for the dust to settle so they could see what had happened below.

Tyson coughed as he realized that he was alive.

What happened? He remembered running at his dad, and then a collision, then nothing. Tyson also realized he was buried under the dirt and snow. He must be hurt, he thought. The area must have collapsed on top of him.

Yet, he didn't feel any pain. In fact, he felt strong. Tyson began digging himself out, pushing at the snow and dirt around him. It surprised him how strong he felt, and how easily the debris moved away as he pushed at it. Where was this strength coming from?

At last he reached an open space, and there was light shining through. He pulled himself out of the dirt and stood up. The air was thick with dust and debris, and he had a difficult time seeing anything.

Slowly the dust settled and Tyson saw someone standing nearby. The dust-covered shape held the long dark stick with both hands.

The two stood there, realizing that they had both survived the collision and collapse, apparently unhurt.

Blade spoke first. "I asked you to join me, and instead you chose your friends."

"You killed my mother!"

"I am your father."

"You may have my father's body, but you are not my father," replied Tyson.

"Join me. You see how powerful we are. No one can touch us if we are together."

"Never," said Tyson. "You are possessed by the evil of that stick. Drop it, and join me."

"Our power comes from the stick; I am not giving

this up."

Kenny and Casey could hear voices coming from below. The looked down again and could see the two figures.

"Tyson is alive," said Kenny.

"So is his father," answered Casey.

"Kenny," said White Crane. "Come here."

Kenny and Casey both walked over and knelt down.

"You must help Tyson get the stick out of his father's hands. You cannot fail. You must save him. We need him to help us. The father cannot die."

"Got it," said Kenny. He was feeling stronger now. "Any suggestions?"

"Yes. You cannot fight him directly. He is too powerful. Use your flight. Fly, hit, and move away. The claw at the end of your stick will work to latch onto his stick. It can break the hold he has on the stick when you are close. Use it."

"Alright, got it," said Kenny.

Kenny walked over to the edge and flew down. Casey walked over to the edge to watch. "Tell me how he does," said White Crane.

Tyson knew talking was not going to get his father to cooperate, but maybe it would give Kenny and the others time to come help. *Hey where are you guys?*

Kenny's mind raced as he flew towards Blade. He really wanted to discuss a plan of action with Tyson before trying to knock the evil stick out of Blade's hands. If he could just knock Blade over and cause him some pain, maybe that would be enough for now. Blade had his back to him, so Kenny had the advantage of surprise. He started to formulate his plan.

He repeated in his mind what White Crane had told him. *Fly, hit, and move away. Fly, hit, and move away.* That was it. He'd hit. He'd hit at the back of Blade's legs, knock him down, and hopefully buy enough time to talk to Tyson.

He pulled back the owl stick and swung it hard. WHAMMM!

Down went Blade, and Kenny reached the ground and ran to Tyson.

"Nice hit," said Tyson.

"We have to get the stick away from him," said Kenny, trying to catch his breath.

"I asked," Tyson grinned sarcastically. "He said

no."

Kenny told Tyson the tips from White Crane and then flew into the air. Again, Blade had recovered and was now the angry one in the group. He was outnumbered and was out in the open.

Kenny flew back in, but Blade turned in time to keep him back. Tyson ran at Blade, who just rolled onto his back and lifted Tyson up and over him, throwing him some thirty feet.

Nice move, thought Kenny.

Kenny looked around, thinking he needed some help. He wanted some fire rocks. However, they were all buried in the landslide. Kenny then remembered that when they'd first arrived, White Crane had to wait for Kenny to arrive because his sack of rocks was on Kenny's snowmobile.

Kenny looked up to the top of the mine. It was quite a distance. Should he try? Could he reach the rocks and return in time to help?

Finally he decided that the longer he considered it the less time he was going to have. So, with a quick burst, he flew towards the edge of the mine. As he neared the top he could see there was no damage up there. He flew right to the snowmobiles and grabbed the sack of rocks.

Flying back he could see Tyson still fighting off his father. *Hold on*, thought Kenny. *Almost there.*

Kenny landed behind Tyson, dropping the rocks onto the ground. "We got some ammo now."

"Thought you left me again," said Tyson.

"Let's finish this. I've got the back side."

Kenny flew up behind Blade and threw a fireball. WHAMMM!

That caught his attention. Blade knew he was out-gunned now. He looked back to Tyson and saw a fireball coming right at him. With a quick reaction Blade deflected it. Kenny swooped down and collected another one and took another shot, this time at Blades legs, but Blade jumped and avoided the shot.

As quickly as Blade turned back around, Tyson had another one coming. This time his attempt to deflect missed and Tyson watched as his father fell back. Tyson ran over and with his polar bear stick used the claw end to rip the evil stick out of his dad's hands.

The stick went flying into the air. Kenny just missed colliding with it as he returned to the ground. *I've got to get that stick away from here! It's the only way to make it safe for all of us!*

Tyson first went to check on his dad. Blade's jacket was still smoldering. Tyson reached down and patted out the remaining embers. He looked into his dad's eyes, and saw that the flame-look was now missing. Blade's eyes closed as he passed out.

Kenny walked over to where the evil polar bear stick had fallen. The black bone shaft looked unhurt from all the fighting, hitting, and explosions. It seemed so calm and harmless just lying there on the ground.

"What do we do with it?" asked Tyson.

"How's your dad?" asked Kenny.

"I think he'll be okay. That weird fire look is gone from his eyes."

"Good. I should ask White Crane what to do with the stick."

Kenny bent down to take flight when he heard Casey call out, "Someone is coming!"

Kenny and Tyson both looked up towards the top of the mine. Sure enough, headlights could be seen coming down the spiral road. They watched as the visitors navigated the tricky path that had collapsed earlier.

"It's Koti and Journey," said Casey.

Journey signaled for Koti and Lonni to go down

to the boys, while he went to meet White Crane and Casey.

"Decided to join us after all?" asked White Crane dryly.

"Figured you might need some help finding your way back," said Journey.

"Tyson did it," said White Crane. "He got his dad back."

Journey did a half smile, and looked around for Yuraa. He looked down below and over to Casey.

"Yuraa?" he asked.

Casey turned away. She did not want to answer that question. Journey turned to White Crane.

"I'm sorry," said White Crane. "She has fallen."

Down below, Koti and Lonni reached Tyson and Kenny. "Someone needs a bath," teased Lonni.

Kenny and Tyson didn't really respond. Kenny saw that even with their victory, it would be Tyson's mom not returning with them today.

"Tyson's mom...," said Kenny, but he did not finish.

Koti and Lonni turned to Tyson, then looked around. They realized something bad had happened.

Journey called down, "White Crane needs to get

back immediately. Lonni, you should go to Blade and load him onto your sled."

Journey looked around again and asked, "Where's Yuraa?"

"She was buried by the landslide. Down there," pointed Casey.

Journey called down again, "We will send others to help bring everyone home."

Koti realized that he meant everyone, including Tyson's mom.

Kenny asked, "What should I do with the stick?"

"Bring it back with you, but do not directly touch the dark stick. We shall decide what to do with it in the morning," said Journey.

Flamethrowers II

25

Deep in the heart of

The next morning Kenny woke, feeling the many adventures from the prior day in every muscle of his body. As he stretched, he heard voices coming from the kitchen. He wandered in to join Casey, Journey, and Koti as they talked.

Tyson joined next and he was dragging too, looking as though he hadn't slept yet.

"How's your dad?" asked Casey.

"He's not awake yet," answered Tyson. The cracking in his voice and the redness in his eyes showed everyone that he must have been crying most of the night. Tyson left the kitchen and returned to his father's side.

No one could imagine how it must have felt to be him. Losing a brother, his father leaving, and then finding his father only to lose his mother. Tyson's emotions were his. Only he was going to walk this path to recovery.

White Crane entered the kitchen with the others. He moved slowly and grabbed the back of the chairs as he hobbled his way around the table.

"Good to see you up my friend," said Journey.

"Good to be seen my friend," he replied.

Casey leaned over to White Crane, "I'm glad you're alive too. I'm sorry for wanting the stick."

"Casey, we each have our own destiny," said White Crane. "You are an important piece in our quest."

The group returned to silence, feeling their pains from the prior day. Tyson could be heard in the adjoining room, "Dad. Dad."

"How is Blade?" asked White Crane.

"He was hurt pretty bad, like yourself," said Journey. "Lonni stitched you two up pretty good."

"Dad!" cried out Tyson. "He's awake."

The group in the kitchen came into the room to

see Tyson kneeling in front of his dad, who was on the couch.

"He's awake!" repeated an excited Tyson.

Blade had opened his eyes and was looking around. He looked like a person who had no idea where he was, and no idea who most of these people were.

"Dad," sighed Tyson as he placed his head on Blade's chest to hug him.

Blade continued to look around. He recognized his son Tyson, but no one else.

"What's going on?"

"We rescued you from the mine," said Tyson.

"Rescued?" questioned Blade.

"How long had you been out there?" asked Journey.

"Too long," said Blade. "Been fighting the demons too long."

"I wish I knew you were so close," said Tyson.

"I've watched you grow up," said Blade. "Helped you a few times when you did some stupid stuff too."

Tyson was confused, "I haven't seen you in years."

"Remember the time you attacked the polar

bear?"

Tyson nodded.

"That was me that carried you home to your mother."

Tyson hugged him again.

"Speaking of your mother, where is she?"

The excitement that had been building in the room suddenly left. Blade looked around and no one was looking at him, all eyes were staring down at the ground.

"What happened? Where is she?" he asked.

Tyson's eyes filled with tears as he looked at his dad. Blade's eyes began to fill up too, as he anticipated what Tyson was about to tell him. Tyson shared the whole story. The group watched as Tyson explained about the evil stick and the curse that it held. None of them felt any blame towards Blade.

Blade slowly sat up and walked to the window. He stared out at the newly fallen snow and at the dark morning sky. What had he done?

For several minutes the group was silent, letting all of the news sink in. Blade then turned and walked over to Tyson. "I have you son. We have each other. I am sorry for not being here for you."

Tyson hugged his father and Blade looked at

Journey and the others. Blade tried to smile as he said, "I believe some introductions are needed."

Journey said, "Ah yes. I believe you have met my son Koti and daughter Lonni before."

Blade had not seen them in years and nodded his head towards them.

"We have visitors from Minnesota. White Crane, Casey, and Kenny."

"Where are these sticks you mentioned," Blade asked Tyson.

Tyson walked over to grab the good polar bear stick. He handed it to his father. "This is the safe one."

Blade looked at the baby blue stick made from bone and fur. He was still struggling with accepting the story, but he also had no reason to doubt anyone in the room.

"What are you going to do with it?" asked Blade.

"I don't know," said Tyson, turning to Journey and White Crane. "What is it we do next?"

Journey approached Tyson and looked him in the eyes. "You will go with White Crane to help the next person acquire the Flamethrower stick."

"I am not leaving my father," said Tyson. "I just got him back and I am not going anywhere."

"You have a duty now," said Journey.

"I don't owe anyone anything. I didn't ask for this," said Tyson.

Blade stepped in to defend his son. "We belong together now. You cannot ask Tyson to join some quest."

White Crane stepped forward. "Blade, you must come too. You have experienced something none of us have. You held the evil stick for a very long time. You bonded with it, you know what it wants."

"I don't remember anything," pleaded Blade.

"You will," answered White Crane. "And there is much we can learn from you. Your insight can help us understand our enemy."

Tyson and Blade looked at each other. *At least we will be together* they thought.

"Where do we need to go?" asked Tyson.

"Texas," answered White Crane.

"What's in Texas?" asked Casey.

"The scorpion stick," said White Crane. "There is a girl who needs our help."

Tyson nodded and turned to his dad. "Together, right?"

Blade nodded, "I love you, son."

That evening the group held a service for Yuraa. The group held hands and sang.

As the service came to an end, Casey looked up to see the streaks and ribbons of green, yellow, and blue.

"Look, the Northern Lights are out," she said.

The group all looked up and marveled at the lights dancing across the sky.

Casey asked, "Isn't it a bit early in the season to see the Northern Lights?"

White Crane nodded, "Those are lacrosse players in the next world playing for us. Death does not stop lacrosse."

Flamethrowers II

About the Author

J. Alan Childs lives in Savage, Minnesota. He is married with five mostly-grown lacrosse kids, with five granddaughters, soon to be lacrosse players.

His prior works include:
- Flamethrowers Volume 1
- Minnesota Lacrosse: A History
- Flamethrower Stories:
  Which team do I play for? *(Picture book)*
- Lacrosse History Trivia Card game

Keep up with him at laxhistorygeek.com
Email: flamethrowerprod@gmail.com
Facebook.com/Flamethrowerlax

Made in the USA
San Bernardino, CA
14 December 2016